"Rebecca is person of high integrity. She brings light, passion, and years of experience to uncovering the secrets of true belonging—being home with who you are, where you are."

—Stephanie Bennett Vogt,
founder of SpaceClear and
author of *Your Spacious Self*

"Don't you want to feel as if you belong wherever you are? I do, and this exquisite book is an intriguing map to thinking yourself home. I felt like Alice in Wonderland as I tumbled through its pages, more and more curious as I explored the inner and outer environments that make up the world in which I choose to live and belong."

—Dawna Markova, author of
I Will Not Die an Unlived Life
www.ptpinc.org

"*Being Home* is a wonderful book of both practical and deeply meaningful advice on how to find the sense of home we are all looking for in every aspect of our lives. It will get you asking if the things you own support or drain you, help you let go of those for which the answer is the latter, and simultaneously give you the tools to take an accurate self-assessment of your real priorities. Ross uses her experience as an organizational consultant, along with her training as an architect, to bring structure and order to the process of finding an inner orientation to the environments we inhabit—from house, to body, to self. A deeply spiritual book, it will provide you with a set of simple techniques for finding that sense of being home, no matter where you are."

—Sarah Susanka, author of
The Not So Big Life and
The Not So Big House series

BEING HOME

BEING HOME

THE ART OF BELONGING
WHEREVER YOU ARE

REBECCA ROSS

**TURNING
STONE
PRESS**

Cover design by Frame25 Productions
Cover art by Shutterstock © Angela Waye
Illustrations by James Nielsen, www.reservenote.tumblr.com
Author photo by Ingrid Pape-Sheldon Photography
Interior design by Jane Hagaman

Turning Stone Press
8301 Broadway St. Ste. 422
San Antonio TX, 78209
turningstonepress.com

Library of Congress Cataloging-in-Publication Data available upon request.

ISBN 978-1-61852-098-2

10 9 8 7 6 5 4 3 2 1

Printed in the United States of America

Contents

Introduction

Approaching Home

Home, for the coyotes, is always the same, only in a new place. It is different for humans. Home is harder to locate, if you set out to find it.

—*Home: Chronicle of a North Country Life,*
by Beth Powning

In her book *Life Would Be Perfect if I Lived in That House,* Meghan Daum describes her lifelong search for a place that meets an ideal she calls "domestic integrity." By this she means living in a place that perfectly reflects the person dwelling in it, an indefinable acknowledgment of belonging. She moves repeatedly, each time hoping for the perfect place with the right tile, view, or ceiling height. Each time, she quickly or gradually becomes dissatisfied, while ignoring her own intuition. The very last paragraph in the book captures the challenge perfectly:

Maybe learning how to be out in the big world isn't the epic journey everyone thinks it is. Maybe that's actually the easy part. The hard part is what is right in front of you. The hard part is learning how to hold the title to your very existence, to own not only property, but also your life. The hard part is learning not just how to be, but mastering the nearly impossible art of how to be at home.

Difficult and elusive perhaps, but not impossible. There is a skill set, a process of listening to yourself that can be learned, and applying these skills is the core of *Being Home*.

Stairways have always beckoned me upward and around corners; open doorways, unexpected nooks, and anything hidden could draw me into places the grown-ups wished I'd leave alone. At about age nine, my interest in rooms and buildings eventually led me to ask, "Who gets to think up such places?" The glamorous occupation of "architect" sounded like a good way to both support myself and have fun creating marvelous rooms, so my future was settled.

The reality of the profession was another story. Architects are expected to put in vast amounts of time and attention for relatively low pay. Very few reach the level of prosperity I had imagined, and I wanted a more balanced life. Much later, as a single mother of two children, with other interests and priorities, I just wasn't that dedicated. Work felt more like a drain than a career, and I began to look for ways out.

When feng shui arrived on the West Coast in the early 1990s, it seemed like a great way to connect people to their environments. It addresses this quality of energy that is found in rooms, sometimes called qi or chi in Chinese, in a practical way. However, after some study and exploration, I saw it being used as a set of superficial prescriptions and cures. People were installing mirrors or wind chimes because a book said to, without understanding the differences between them, or their real impact.

At the beginning of its popularity there was no mention of why or how these "cures" worked—or the role of the person in the equation. Over the years, I've met some dedicated and skilled feng shui practitioners who did install cures and explained how they worked, but at the time, I wanted something with less formula and that was more intuitive. These pieces finally came together when I founded the Composed Domain.

I created the business called "The Composed Domain" in 2000, a child born of several different parents. One parent was personal organizing, helping people with their clutter and overwhelming paperwork. Seeing this process open up the world for my clients, giving them space to function and enjoy their homes, was deeply satisfying. But I wanted to understand how I was able to "read" what each space needed for the change.

The other parent was discovered by taking classes from a number of teachers about energetic space clearing. I met people who were talking about the subjective qualities of a space: how it felt to them and how to adjust the feeling of a specific room. The combination of these disciplines was still missing an important element, which didn't become clear until I began learning more about personal energetics. The words *energy* and *energetic* may seem either too broad or too ill-defined, but they serve as handles for systems of information that have both visceral and measurable effects on your experience in places and with people.

Personal energetics are simply another sensory mechanism, no more esoteric or paranormal than your ability to see, hear, smell, or recognize the contents of the room you're sitting in right now. In fact, you have an energetic anatomy that can be developed to perceive and interact with this information all around you. In the marriage of these parents, the practical and the subjective, a link is created. Making this connection is something that you can learn to do and it's at the heart of your ability to come home to your own dwelling.

A room that is meant to be a bedroom may not always feel like a restful place. Part of the problem may be obvious. It could be a color that reminds you of a disco, or a window that overlooks a busy street. Paint and sound-baffling curtains could fix the surface problems, but there may be other issues. If your bedroom is the setting for endless nights of insomnia, you may need to heal your relationship to the room itself. In order to do this, you'll need to recognize how you are affected by the room, and how to find your own balance, there and anywhere. Only then can you bring the room back into alignment with yourself and your need for a good night's sleep.

The goal is to live in a supportive and meaningful place that reflects what really matters to you. What does this look and feel like?

Being Home teaches you practical skills for body awareness and for improving the feeling of safety, control, and function in your rooms. Your ability to be more aware can serve you at home, work, and out in the world. I'll also be referring you to books and sources that have fed my thinking and that you may want to explore further. I invite you to step across the threshold into a conscious relationship with all the places where you live.

How does this relationship between you and your belongings affect your day-to-day life? You can count on finding tools for daily living when you need them. You'll know exactly what you have in your closets, and that you love wearing all of it. You'll enjoy looking at decorations and treasures that reflect your past, present, and future interests. When you go out into the world, you'll trust that you can navigate unfamiliar circumstances and places with confidence and pleasure. And then you'll come home to a place that enfolds and nourishes you. Your real home reveals itself, right here.

Chapter 1

What Is Home?

A tourist from America paid a visit to a renowned Polish rabbi, Hofetz Chaim. He was astonished to see the rabbi's home was only a simple room filled with books, plus a table and bench.

"Rabbi," asked the tourist, "Where is your furniture?"

"Where is yours?" replied the rabbi.

The puzzled American asked, "Mine? But I am only passing through."

"So am I," said Hofetz Chaim.

—*Tales of the Hassidim,* by Martin Buber

Being at home is more than physical comfort and peace of mind. When your body, mind, and the physical places you inhabit are connected to your *being*, you can begin to find home anywhere you are. By living in your spaces and your life fully, you'll express and expand your most true self, no matter where you go. When you step into a new relationship with your surroundings, you profoundly and directly improve your sense of well-being and vitality. With these goals in mind, I invite you to reinvent your own backdrop for living.

This invitation opens a door to new choices. As you cross the threshold, you come home not only to your environment, but also to your own thinking and emotional balance. In the process, you will acquire awareness about what it means to come home to your own body, self, and space.

Begin with the willingness to ask a powerful question: what will it take to live and work in spaces that feel just right?

Home is a place where you belong, can rest, feel safe, and recharge in a secure environment. What exactly does it take to feel at home, to know that place reflects what matters to you? Not everyone grew up in a comfortable house or had the chance to decorate a childhood bedroom. Was it even possible to find a safe nook of your own? Understanding the home you live in now may require looking back. Did the adults around you take care of their surroundings, or were things chaotic, unsettled? In an ideal world, you spend your time in a place that reflects your taste, is comfortable, and functions well. Even if this is not the case, you're in a relationship with the place you live, whether you know it or not.

Exile: An Experience of Identity Separated from Place

Home is also an idea that usually conjures a sense of ownership and belonging. Whatever your personal stories may be, if you haven't found that place or are separated from it by circumstance, you may feel exiled. And sometimes it isn't about the physical circumstances. Even living in a lovely house in a city of your choice, if you have not found home in your own body and self, you may still feel untethered, slightly off kilter, displaced somehow.

Eva Hoffman moved as a child with her family from Poland to Canada and writes of her own detachment and the sense of loss that followed in her book *Lost in Translation*. Part of her personal challenge was the search for balance in a land offering so much material abundance that it seemed impossible ever to be satisfied. She calls it the "land of yearning." It's a place where opportunity presents people with so many possibilities that there is no way to settle for what they have or, most important, who they are.

Hoffman's Polish friends see identity or character as a given, something one simply has without question. For them, outside circumstances explain their feelings or reactions. The drama of life is external, and their stories are about what happens. Her friends in North America focus instead on their internal experiences and struggle to explain it all in terms of their own particular and individual psychology.

Like "pilgrims of internal progress," some people feel responsible for constant improvement and self-management. Hoffman's Polish friends think the Americans aren't facing simple reality with their endless self-analysis. An American might explain: *I am having intense self-worth issues, my job is soulless, and I need to create.* A more European and pointed statement might be: *I choose to quit my soulless job and am moving to Paris.* The Poles' direct, fact-telling mode can seem blunt and withholding of an emotional component to an American wanting the inside story of feelings and introspection.

Which is more real? Both approaches depend on the relationship between your identity or sense of self and the circumstances of your surroundings. Both reflect ways to handle the outside world, and the more you understand your own assumptions about that process, the more likely you'll feel at home there. Exile is being separated from a country, a house, a family, or anything that signifies belonging. Even in a world you have carefully arranged, you can feel exiled if you aren't at home in your own mind and emotions. The phrase "make yourself at home" points to more than taking your shoes off. Only you can make your *self* a home, and from there create that rest, ease, and belonging in the places you live, work, and sleep. It's a relationship and requires communication.

EXERCISE
Start the Conversation

Invite your bedroom . . . or wherever you sleep . . . to speak to you. Go into the room and find a comfortable place to sit and, if possible, close the door. Have paper and pen or a device nearby to record your exchange.

- How does the room sustain you? With clothing, pillows, books, a clock? Make a list. Include what you enjoy about it: the colors, the art or objects.

- When you go to bed, are you able to let go of the day easily? What are your typical routines in the space, and are they really restful?

- When you get up again, are you ready and able to launch into the day with ease?

- If the room does not feel supporting, list why. Noises, temperature, or a bad mattress? Try to identify anything that feels wrong or uncomfortable.

Now imagine not having this place—if you were detained in a distant airport, or the building burned down, or if you were living on someone's sofa or on the street.

- How does that feel? What would you miss most?

- Does this idea trigger any gratitude or appreciation for what is here now?

- Or perhaps you experience a sense of freedom, escape, or release?

The place you sleep in has its own identity, and you can communicate with it about its gifts or shortcomings. Your reactions to these questions show what you bring to the relationship.

- How do you talk to this place? What would you like to say to it?
- How do you tend to your sleeping place? By providing blankets, lights, hangers?
- Listen for its messages about what feels right or what needs to be fixed.

There is a vivid difference between a "home" and a "place you sleep at night." The latter could be a hotel room or a campground with little or no personal meaning. Your home is the expression of the connection between your mind, feelings, sense of self, and the external, physical world. A home is far more complex, reflecting that correspondence. It is a dance in which your awareness can directly shape the rooms you live in. This might be as simple as putting your clothes away, or as complex as moving to a place with more natural light.

Learning this dance requires openness to both past and present circumstances. You may have to let go of old patterns and things that once felt safe, but aren't working anymore. The relationship between your inner and outer worlds will evolve no matter how fast or slowly the changes happen. The point is to step into the flow and take the lead. By engaging with the dance, you can learn how to inhabit not just your bedroom, but the wider world as well.

Nested Ways of Being Home

Every house, apartment, condo, ashram, or dorm you've ever lived in is seen through the lens of your emotional and intellectual being. You enter each of these places in your physical body with its sensations, reactions, and general state of health. The rooms, filled with your belongings and accumulated history, are another layer in this nested series of places. In turn, you move through the world of nature, cities, streets, and encounters with other people.

The challenge is to recognize each layer and take ownership. The link between these layers is your *being*. As a word this fits quite well, because it's both an object and an action. With the attention of your *being* on each of these nested places you can, by consciously *being*, create a meaningful environment within all of these layers. The following illustrations present the way awareness of these nests can take you from the idea of taking a walk, to the experience itself.

Internal Home: Your inner/mental world of self, personality, and identity. With comfort in your deepest core, self-awareness, and presence, you can know what matters at each of the other nested layers.

The nest of your inner being holds your idea of self in the world.

Body Home: Your external/physical world of body and health. Pleasure in the ownership of your body and health creates your vehicle for action, and it becomes the tool for creating your home.

The nest of your body is vital to being where you are and want to be.

Spatial Home: Your rooms and spaces that hold your belongings, memories, and tools. The space in which you eat, sleep, bathe, and pay bills is another framework for being. It becomes a place that expresses and supports you, in turn expanding your sense of how to be at home in the world.

The nest of your home serves the goals
and dreams of your innermost nested self.

Nature Home: Your relationship to nature as a source of inspiration, healing, and grounding. The natural world provides a living context and backdrop for being home. It supports you in finding balance; it can both stimulate and soothe.

The nest of nature is always there to be explored and honored.

Expanded Home: Your world of streets, stores, workplace, recreation and other people. Being at home in self, body, nature, and environment, you carry a sense of relaxed and alert presence with you everywhere.

The nest of larger world is yours, an extension of the home you create.

Example: The Grocery Store

How do the nested layers fit together? Take a simple, everyday trip to the market. You bring your mood, the day's schedule, and other priorities into the process of shopping. In the market itself, you'll encounter brightly colored signs and all sorts of stimulating situations. The building will be full of people with their own moods and attitudes. Your state of mind is affected by all of these factors, the attitudes of the checker, or perhaps an adventure with the automatic scanner. And you, in turn, affect that checker and the people behind you in line.

Your sense of personal well-being, flexibility, or degree of patience all create ripples in the environment. Then you return to the car with traces of the market in your mind and body. There is constant flow between all these nested layers of place, and learning to recognize and manage them gives you greater control over what and how much is affecting you.

The total picture of all this information and your reaction to it can be called the perceived *energy* of the place. Once you begin to recognize that you've always been engaged with it at some level, it can become a conscious tool. In later chapters, you'll learn how this energetic content can be adjusted, or "cleared," for your comfort and personal goals.

Knowing and understanding how you relate to the energy of the market can make a big difference in the efficiency and pleasure of your shopping trip and how you feel when you're unloading the groceries at home. This increased awareness is a radical skill in being right where you are. It's the hallmark of finding home wherever you stand.

Home as a Map of the Mind and a Reflection of the Self

On some deep level, we all know that our belongings are a reflection of who we are. These things don't sneak into our homes in the night while we're asleep. We've gradually surrounded ourselves with objects for many different reasons, and before any change can occur we must take stock. The challenge is profound, since we have cluttered up our heads at the same time we have brought our belongings into our space. We hold on to so many ideas and beliefs about the objects that we become our own biggest obstacle. Being home includes questioning these stories and reasons.

Examining our thinking can start to free us from objects and create more space for change. This is true no matter how much actual stuff we have. A college student in her first dorm room or the owner of a three-car garage full to the rafters: both these people face relationships with a space that can be acknowledged and healed.

It is possible that they are struggling with simple clutter or a sense that nothing they own really fits or reflects their taste. Too many hand-me-downs or make-do furnishings might be distracting. Creating an environment that is "just right" is not about time, money, or decorating talent. When a person finds home in their own body and self, it is easier to design a room that reflects a feeling of belonging.

What is being home to me? What does it mean to be held by a space, knowing I am home? After a day out in the world, I need to know that I am safe, welcomed, and that the room will hold me and everything I bring with me. How my office functions, the objects and furniture, are surface qualities. What matters is how it feels when I walk in. Walking in, I need a place to set down my bags and coat. I'll want to put my phone on the desk, next to the mail. Next comes the moment of being held by my space. My whole day, with all its events and interactions, can be brought in and be handled, processed, and let go. It's safe and easy to drop both my shoes and my concerns into a trusted place.

Looking around, I'm surrounded by my own choices. Everything in the office was chosen and placed in a spot that works. The books speak from the shelves, the colors delight my eyes, and there's my familiar, comfortable chair. I know exactly where things are; it's easy to fuss around and answer email, find stamps, or catch up on paperwork. Held by my office, I can sit down and process my day or do nothing at all, watch the birds in the garden, and feel the welcome sense of being in my domain. This is my birthright as a human being—to grow in awareness and the ability to shape my world.

Being Home Whether You Are at Home or Not

When I'm truly at home in myself, I can function in the wider world with ease and patience. In this condition, it's clear that I'm responsible for my experience. It's a way of *being* that accepts the reality of any current situation and cuts through stories that don't serve me or anyone else.

Let's say I just missed the bus. My opinion of this event will dictate my emotional reaction. Is it a calamity or an inconvenience? Being at home in my mind and body makes it possible to move from reaction to choice. Shall I just settle back and wait for the next bus, or do I hail a cab? What are my real options? Do I have to start making phone calls to arrange a ride? If the next bus is thirty minutes away and I have my book, waiting is no problem. But if I'm already late for a meeting, corrective action is required. Quick, call for that ride or hail a cab!

Being at home in mind, body, and place allows me to see, understand, and relate to circumstances and other people. When I trust myself in any situation, I can interact with accurate vision and compassion. Without inhabiting my own senses fully, none of these things are likely. By dwelling here, I navigate the nested homes of body, mind, self, and space with ease and grace.

How do you get to this place? In order to feel at home in yourself, as well as your body-home, not to mention the bedroom, you need to know where you are right now. This requires awareness and presence, and I invite you to open the door and step inside the dwelling of your own awareness.

Chapter 2

Open the Door
Creating Awareness

If you have really learned how to think, how to pay attention, then you will know you have other options. It will actually be within your power to experience a crowded, loud, slow, consumer-hell-type situation as not only meaningful but sacred, on fire with the same force that lit the stars . . . compassion, love, the sub-surface unity of all things. Not that the mystical stuff's necessarily true: the only thing that's capital T True is that you get to decide how you're going to see it. You get to decide what has meaning and what doesn't.

—From "David Foster Wallace on Life and Work,"
Kenyon College commencement speech, 2005

Wallace was a complicated guy. Brilliant and eccentric, an author and philosopher, he committed suicide before his last book was published. For me, the power of his observation stands. In the same address quoted above, he went on to talk about the idea that people get to choose what matters and what to worship. His theory was that we all worship something, and he recommended something like God, Allah, Yahweh, the Four Noble Truths, or some other spiritual or ethical principle. In his experience, worshipping something like money, things, or worldly power could be a problem because ". . . they will eat you alive." For Wallace, ". . . if this is where you tap real meaning in life you will never have enough."

Wallace kicks off the speech with this short story:

> There are these two young fish swimming along, and they happen to meet an older fish swimming the other way, who nods at them and says, "Morning, boys, how's the water?" And the two young fish swim on for a bit, and then eventually one of them looks over at the other and goes, "What the hell is water?"

The talk concludes with:

> Awareness of what is so real and essential, so hidden in plain sight all around us, that we have to keep reminding ourselves over and over: this is water, this is water. It is unimaginably hard to do this, to stay conscious and alive, day in and day out.

Knowing what we do about his later choices, I feel touched and sad that this mind is no longer with us. But the water is still everywhere I look.

EXERCISE
Where Are You and How Does This Place Feel?

You are the only instrument available for this task, and in order to make any changes, you must pay attention. Is the

chair comfortable, the room warm, are you in the car waiting, or has a breeze just riffled these pages? Take a moment
and examine your immediate sense of your surroundings. Is it
open and spacious, cozy and protected, or clinical and cold?
Are you in public, in motion, or in nature? It's easy to make
judgments about a place based on your current agenda or
needs in the moment.

As you practice awareness of where you are, try to let
these concerns go, and instead make a mental or written list
of only what is right there. Rather than focusing only on the
stoplight that is taking forever to change, notice the people
next to you, the signage across the street, the birds on the
wires overhead.

If you feel "not at home," it's important to understand why. A
chair that is too close to the carpet edge or a bookcase crammed
beyond capacity is a message. It communicates a piece of information. The content will affect people in different ways. Does
it make you want to twitch the chair back onto the carpet and
donate a few books? For someone else, the slight disarray is perfect for a relaxed evening. These cues are there, waiting to be read.
They can be seen in the furniture layout of a waiting room, the
curving paths in an arboretum, or the roundabout intersection
you navigate in your car.

The point is to become aware of what this information is saying
to *you*. This is called reading your environment. You do it all the
time, in grocery store lines and when picking out a seat in a restaurant, and it's practically automatic. When it becomes a conscious
skill set, you can create and sustain a deep trust that you are "being
home."

The following examples are taken from real people who recognized and faced issues in their homes. I will be changing names and
combining some of the details in order to protect my sources and
illustrate points.

Helen: Paper Jam

Information pours into our mailboxes, computers, and smart-phones, surrounding us on all sides. We carry it home in purses, pockets, and children's backpacks. Unless a clear and simple system is in place for processing all this paper or digital information, it not only piles up, but tends to breed when we aren't looking.

Helen, a busy mother of two, was employed full time; she had a supportive husband and a lovely home. She also had more paper and interesting things to read than the hours of a week could hold and nowhere to keep what mattered.

Keeping paper involves filing; this is the reality she didn't want to face. A decade of helping people with paper has convinced me that unless you know your own mind, you won't be able to file anything. Before any system could be designed, it was crucial for Helen to think about the categories of information she was keeping. And even more important: what was her relationship to that information?

Paper and email stack up because it's hard to make decisions, and if we believe that we must keep and attend to the flow of data, it feels like we're drowning in it. When Helen began to ask herself where she really wanted to put her effort and time, it became possible to let go of paper that had previously seemed important. She decided that catalogs could stand vertically in a box only big enough for current issues. This way they are easy to use and recycle when the next ones come. Next she set up a place to put the children's art, right where they unload their backpacks.

Her relationship with the catalogs and artwork shifted and instead of feeling tangled up in information overload, the paper and all it held began to flow again. Flowing is what information and paper should do! Helen found it liberating to come home to her own mind and adjust her environment to mirror it.

Joan: Reclaiming a Room and a Life

Hoarding is an extreme example of a relationship in trouble. My client Joan had reached this point, and at the urging of her family members set up an organizing assessment. Her home had become a network of paths between mounds of objects, with small nests for sleeping and eating. I could see clear evidence of her interests mingled in the stacks: lots of valuable family mementos, craft supplies, and musical instruments. In amongst these things were also past pull-date food, broken appliances, and dirty clothing. We began the work slowly and limited our focus to her living room.

Before touching a single object, we established that the goal was not "cleaning up a room" but "reclaiming a life." The stuff surrounding Joan had made everyday functioning difficult, and the pressure from her family to make a change was growing. How could we create a safe place for Joan to make different decisions about each and every object surrounding her?

At the heart of each and every choice was Joan herself. She learned to recognize that her home is not defined by things and all the stories about them; her home is within her body and being. This is not a matter of willpower or "just doing it"; a huge transformation of focus is required. By getting some things out the door, space opens up, and what steps in to take residence is a being who lives there. Beneath the boxes of stray dishes and odd remnants of craft projects, we discovered artwork by family members that found a new home on the fireplace mantel. Now Joan can see and enjoy the special mementos and hear the stories they tell with meaningful voices.

Each hoarding situation is individual and complicated. It can start with a trauma or be a long, slow accumulation of objects. Therapy with a qualified professional is necessary to understand the situation and make lasting changes.

Your Attention, Please: If You Don't Have Control of It, Something Else Has Taken It

A lot has been written about "the law of attraction" and the power of the mind to shape experience. Some popular books focus on getting what you want in the material and financial areas of life, and others address life experiences that can be attained and adjusted with the skills of attention. Lynne McTaggart, in her book *The Intention Experiment,* takes it to another level by proposing that conscious intentions shape the world we live in. She states, "thought is a thing that affects other things," and offers exercises for using attention and intention, as well as a platform for tracking actual changes in defined targets.

The bottom line is that if you are not directing your attention, it is being directed for you. It's a matter of recognizing when you give it away! Recipients of your attention might be a billboard, the TV, a novel, or the words of your teenager as she heads out with your car. Worship may be too strong a word for this giving up of our attention, but, still, we often feel as if we are being pressured by the demands on it. It can feel like swimming in a sea of total overload, and who notices the water now?

The process of cultivating awareness in situations can be enhanced with some well-known and time-tested practices. The starting point is always right here, in the bodies we all live in. It took me years to realize I was walking around not in my body but in my head. This attitude is common in a society run by social, economic, and power-driven concerns. Even with a huge premium placed on good looks, our bodies are often treated like shopping carts to carry brains around.

For some of us, our minds process new information first, with feeling coming later, if ever. Other people act on feelings first and neglect to run that information through the tempering of the intellect. In either case, volumes of meaning may be missing. What to trust?

Believing either your intellect or bodily sensations to be infallible is the problem. Being awake in the world means listening to both, recognizing that they each offer clues to what's happening around you. Intellect and body cues both require careful attention in order to determine what is really important.

What is doing this processing? Imagine you are busily dealing with a mental message to change the light bulb and also listening to feedback from a sore shoulder. Where is the balanced decision made to go find a ladder instead of hurting yourself by reaching up? In this example, it may start either place. Perhaps you are attuned to the physical quality of pain around your shoulder and this message triggers the mind; it considers how to avoid further injury by fetching the ladder. That same body message may also cause an emotional reaction of irritation, frustration, or fear.

Or you might typically start from the purely mental strategy of knowing that a ladder will save you from experiencing any pain at all, eliciting a feeling of satisfaction, even pride in your reasonable behavior. Within you is a complex internal dance of information—physical, mental and emotional—and the binding force is your conscious self.

Books about the study of consciousness fill many shelves, and lifetimes have been spent in exploration of awareness—something so close you ignore it. By taking a moment to listen, you can recognize the voice of your internal witness. It speaks to you about the condition of both body and mind, interprets emotions and mental constructs, as well as physical sensations. The witness can be an elusive critter, living beneath the surface of your daily concerns. But then it may snap into focus, filling moments with intense presence: the sudden call of a bird that pierces your heart or that moment of realizing you are standing on a chair reaching for a ceiling fixture.

Techniques to increase such moments and ways to connect with your internal witness have finally reached the mainstream.

There are meditation paths of all kinds, ways to expand personal potential, and physical disciplines that call on awareness: yoga, tai chi, qigong, and so forth. But one class, or even a series, won't be enough. A path is a *practice,* meant to become a part of how you live, like flossing teeth. These techniques all open doorways to the witness, some using stillness and some teaching movement to unite body and mind. They all require you to listen carefully, owning your full attention.

Uniting Awareness and Environment

In this union, you'll find the connecting tissue between the personal awareness of your mind and body and the larger world of information in your environment. But what is the connecting tissue? Since I have not come up with a better word, I will call it energy. "The Force" also works as a handle, since the Jedi knights in the *Star Wars* movies didn't just use it as a source of mastery; they also read data within it about events and places.

Energy exists. We use it all the time, consciously or not. Animals tap into it as a storm approaches, and they take shelter. When you break a bone, the image your doctor uses for a diagnosis is produced by an unseen something—whether it's radiology, ultrasound, or magnetic resonance. Even though we can't directly see the something, we know that it holds and delivers information. The specific qualities and the impact of the energy in your kitchen is much the same. Even though it's hard to quantify or measure these spatial energies, most people have no problem describing their reaction to either a dark alley in a strange city or the inviting sweep of an empty tropical beach.

As a human living inside a body with a mind and a self, you have this incredible capacity to process what exists all around you. How this all happens is the subject of much philosophical and neurological debate. In *Self Comes to Mind: Constructing the Conscious*

Brain, Antonio Damasio defines consciousness as "an organization of mind contents centered on the organism that produces and motivates those contents." He proposes that people labor under a false intuition that mental, emotional business is a fleeting, insubstantial process.

This is likened to pre-Copernican worldviews of the sun revolving around the earth. Damasio is theorizing a more integrated model linking brain, mind, and body in a neurological process that develops over time and results in exactly that witness who manages the ladder, the shoulder pain, and the associated feelings of chagrin and thoughts of efficiency. In one of his chapters, you'll find a reference to the *maps* that are made in consciousness of objects and events in the world around us, as well as maps of the organism of our bodies and feelings. The internal maps are with us always, and while acting on the physical brain, they can also be changed by experience.

Damasio's ideas open the door to understanding how you can use the feedback loop between your inner and outer worlds. Once you understand that these sides of your experience deeply affect one another, it will become a fascinating dance.

In order to wake up to this skill set, you'll need to locate your witness in whatever way makes sense to you. At the fulcrum of a teeter-totter, there is a place to stand that is at the center of movement. All the action can be monitored from here, while you stay balanced. The skills of an awareness practice can help you listen from this place. Here you get cues about your surroundings, the state of your body, and what it might need. You can begin to make meaningful and powerful changes in yourself and your world by listening to both the internal mental dialog and the felt experience of your body at the balanced and centered fulcrum of the witness.

At first, this creates a space between you and your circumstances, but you'll use energetics to monitor and adjust how you relate to places and events. It is not a distancing tool. The ability to track energetically connects you in a more conscious and responsible way. To mix a few metaphors, you'll break out of the locked watchtower of your mind and begin to drive the vehicle of your sensing body.

Once you are able to process the information right here in each circumstance, you can choose what to pay attention to based on your own priorities. So how do you work with this energetic information, sensed with body, mind, and emotions? How do you capture something so hard to measure or objectify? Let's explore some practical and pragmatic situations in which negotiating the energy of a place can ease discomfort, frustration, or feeling overwhelmed.

You can also create more enjoyment of your experience by remembering that you move in a nested series of homes. These layers of being home are fluid and will vary in intensity and importance, with boundaries that depend on your personal style of noticing and taking action. Place yourself in the examples below and identify your way of moving through each place.

EXERCISES
Real World Choices

- *Deciding where to sit in a restaurant:* This is good opportunity to manage your experience in a relaxed and alert way, in either familiar or new places. At the first layer of "being home," enter the room aware of your own internal world; notice if you're already in a stressed mind-set, an open and curious mood, or something in between. Where you sit might help you relax and enjoy the meal, or it could keep you in a state of high alert to a conversation. Second, consider your physical body state and determine how this particular room suits your priorities. Can you locate a comfortable chair facing the window? Will a noisy gang of business people disrupt a quiet conversation? Once you know what matters in this situation, you are in the third layer of home, the external surroundings, as you make these choices. Depending on your options and your ability to navigate them, you have moved to the fourth layer, the social context and your relationship to the wider world. Which of these layers comes first for you?

- **Arranging an office for maximum comfort and efficiency:** Adjustments here depend on understanding how you work. Is a neat desk inspiring or spooky? Are stacks of paper comforting or crazy-making? These assumptions happen at your first, internal layer and determine what happens next. Second, your body will tell you if the chair really works and will provide cues about how important it might be to keep the door shut or open. Once you are at home in mind and body, it's easier to settle the questions of layer three, physical surroundings. Do you prefer stacking in-boxes or an angled wire rack for folders and projects? And when your process with the paper flows, you are again able to connect to the larger world of plans and goals.

- **Enjoying home with fresh senses:** The places we live in can become so familiar that we don't even see the details anymore. Start small, with a typical surface that holds decorations, like a windowsill or fireplace mantel. First remove everything and put it all on a table somewhere else and look at the empty space. This is your backdrop, your blank slate. Look at the items on the table before returning any to the surface you have just cleaned off. How do the objects reflect your internal world? Are the messages still true, interesting, positive, or supportive? How does your body respond to them? A feeling of tiredness or boredom is not a reason to put them back and move on to the crossword puzzle. In fact this is exactly where to question the things—and make a new decision. Your third layer of home, the actual windowsill, now holds what you have chosen to display for real reasons. And finally, when you come home from the busy world, it will be to a place that reflects what matters, supports you, and feels right.

This process is a microcosm of all the choices you make about your surroundings. Skill with stillness, listening, and awareness of energetics help you act on environmental information. You can express your choices in the world and expand your ability to be at home anywhere, under all circumstances.

I would like to conclude this chapter with my own version of David Foster Wallace's challenge to the students he addressed. My source for this paragraph is a letter from a Zen sage named Yuanwu, who was writing to a student sometime in the early 1100s. I have paraphrased the original freely for twenty-first century sensibilities.

When people strive to be aware and cultivate presence in the middle of their regular busy lives, it is like a lotus blooming in the middle of a fire. It's hard to tame the willful desire for success and power, not to mention all the opportunities for frustration involved in "the burning house" of everyday life. The only thing to do is realize for yourself that you are fundamentally real and wondrously whole. This is the way to reach your own place of calm stability.

You've opened a door to radical awareness, and now it's time to step across the threshold.

Chapter 3

Crossing the Threshold
The Nested Layer of Body

I need to remember that my life is, in fact,
a continuous series of thresholds:
from one moment to the next,
from one thought to the next,
from one action to the next. . . .
How many are the chances to be really alive . . .
to be aware of the enormous dimension we live within.

— "Threshold" from *Being Home,* by Gunilla Norris

When you address all the nested layers of being home, you have stepped across a threshold into an enormous dimension of being alive. The sequence of these layers is self, body, nature, personal environment, and the larger world. Each layer is a way of being connected to the world and engaged with it.

If you look at a human life as a cycle, before being home anywhere, we didn't exist! Once we are here, we humans tend to worry so much about not existing that our inevitable death is a topic to be avoided. But we also know that before our birth, this self we so fiercely protect didn't live anywhere. At the risk of sounding existential, it resided in "non-being."

The very first actual place that you inhabit is your mother's womb, where you have a temporary home while your body prepares for the outside world. Once born, you still go through a period of orientation before you can locate yourself in space. Knowing the difference between your own fist and a caregiver's touch is a big step. After months of connection, you gradually come to recognize that there is a separate "me" to explore. Few people consciously remember this transition, probably because managing fingers and toes is a big job. But once you know how to drop a cup, your unique personality steps in to run the show. You are now a being in a body, moving in space.

Life goes on, and you face things like spoons and eventually trikes, and before you really know it, the wide world and all the things in it are here, offering themselves! Some we can control and others not so much. This life can be seen as a cycle, however, and nearing its end you typically find that you're back to the limitations of your body—with joints that ache and eyes that are gradually less than sharp. And from there, whether you're ready or not, non-being waits again. This is reality for the physical vehicle you've been using to get around. Even if your belief and faith say that the self will persist, it will not be wearing this particular set of teeth and skin.

Each of these stages, places, and the passages between them invite your full participation. So how do you recognize them, staying open and able to enjoy and respond to the "burning house of daily life"? Everything you inhabit—mind, body, kitchen, and neighborhood—is in communication with a witness, your *Being*. Now that you are listening, how do you become more skilled, fluent in the language of presence?

Becoming conscious of how you relate to the world and objects starts with how you move about in your body, how it receives and processes information. It requires a realignment of body, mind, and sense of self. This is the beginning of becoming responsible for all experience.

Understanding Your Energetic Anatomy

The tool for reading and responding to the world around you is your body. It is holding this book and taking in information via eyes, ears, or touch. As your physical organs process the information, your mind and being are also weighing the impact of these words and placing them in relationship to your understanding and ideas about reality. In the same way, your surroundings are speaking to you. The human body includes sensing tools that can reach beyond our skin, and this is where you can add to your basic kit of perception. Mark Rich, in his book *Energetic Anatomy*, calls this structure the "human energy system."

By learning to recognize and manage this energetic system, you'll develop a direct connection between your body's knowledge and interior, mental, subjective, and intuitive experience. It will become a feedback loop that informs you in both directions.

This is one of the most fascinating parts of learning to work with this sensing mechanism: people have very different ways of recognizing and relating to the information in the system. Some report seeing changes or patterns with their physical eyes and can describe colors or shapes overlaid on people and objects. Others, me included, do not actually "see," but instead experience vivid images in the mind's eye.

Rich states that perception of energetic structures often involves a combination of the senses such as seeing, or in his case hearing a high-pitched humming, along with a felt impression. For me, there is often a cue in my body: a shiver or spontaneous wave of movement or a tingling in my heels that translates into an overall feeling of increased weightiness. This last sensation may be familiar to you as the experience of becoming more stable, such as a tree might feel with its roots connected into the earth.

Being rooted in your own awareness is a first step towards home.

In addition to body sensations, encounters with energy can trigger distinct changes in mental and emotional states. Think of entering a party full of people you don't know. You may arrive full of excitement and delight at the prospect, but the minute you walk in, it becomes clear that everyone is tense and there is feeling of awkward expectation—and it's not *your* feeling! Once you get further into the room, it becomes obvious that a political argument is raging at the center of a knot of people. *Ah,* you think, *I'll go get a drink and listen before I say anything.* That initial impression can be explained by number of cues (no one greets you, the room's focus is turned inward), but you have in the very first moments "read the energy" of the room. A crucial part of this ability is recognizing when a feeling or impression is *not you.* Without clarity about your own state, and how *you* feel the messages in your environment, this is easy to miss.

Even when there are no obvious clues to be seen or heard, most people can sense a large amount of information about a place, conversation, or social setting. You certainly read body language and take what you see and hear into account, but for those listening intently or learning to tune their energetic receivers, there is always much more. Nonverbal communication can be even more revealing than any words spoken. Using these skills allows you to tap into a very wide continuum of awareness that's available for everyone to use.

How is energetic information received? The mechanisms of perception include physical sensation, hearing, sight, visualization, and listening to internal cues that can occur, such as thoughts or messages. This last category is one I often experience; it feels as if I am receiving a mental download of content, sometimes in words, sometimes as images. Neurological research indicates that some brain activity can be recorded not only before I move, but before I even think consciously about it. This implies that I operate on more than physical input. Part of that is listening to what is all around me, there to be read and understood.

As a human being, I come equipped with this energy-sensing system, whether I develop it or not. Some systems for describing how it works include words from Sanskrit and various disciplines that may feel alien or religious. Mark Rich uses simple words to name these structures in *Energetic Anatomy* and goes into great detail about their functioning, as well as ways to experiment with them. I will describe two of the most basic components, energy centers and fibers, and return to these concepts in later chapters after we lay some more groundwork.

Energy Centers

Commonly known as chakras and found in traditional systems from India and China, energy centers are tools to connect your awareness to different locations in your body. They are typically imagined as circular wheels, or cones, if you think in three dimensions. Anodea Judith, in *Eastern Body, Western Mind*, defines them as "centers of organization that receive, assimilate and express life force energy." While each point is related to a position on the body, they are hard to locate in any verifiable physical tissue. There are said to be nerve ganglion plexuses near each energy center along the spine. In any case, they generate clear, felt sensations to people who cultivate awareness of them.

Consider this: you know you have a liver, but unless you become quite sensitive to its function and condition, you've probably never identified a specific "liver sensation." These nodes or points are also related to the meridians used in acupuncture, another discipline operating with systems in the human body that are hard for Western medicine practitioners to locate to their satisfaction. Even so, practical treatments dealing with meridians and energy centers have been around for centuries and are widely used and respected.

The key thing about these centers is that they govern areas of your *being* that are reflected in body and intellect, as well as your inner emotional and spiritual identity. They are tools for becoming realigned with yourself and your environment. This reflects a traditional understanding that the chakras help you process information coming from the outside world. They are also indicators of how you communicate and participate with your environment. Examples of this process show up in the museum story (p. 36) in particular. For the purpose of *being home,* you should understand that the chakra energy centers are powerful two-way gates to understanding the movement of energy in the body. You can adjust your internal state and use the chakras to read what is happening with the energy around you in the environment.

Start by paying attention to the theoretical location of each chakra in your body. Each point governs an aspect of your energetic anatomy that may or may not be fully functioning.

By learning to attend to these points, you can rebalance them and adjust how you receive information from outside, the impact it has on your system, and your general well-being. The identification and descriptions of the chakras, the overall number of them, and their relationships are defined in many ways by different systems. Most agree that there are points all over the body, some with special qualities that enable you to interact with or sense the environment. The list below is a simplified version to use for expanding skill with your energetic anatomy.

#	Location	Color	Governs	If Imbalanced
0	18" below your feet	Brown	Ability to ground	Feeling off-balance or uncon-nected
1	Base of the spine	Red	Physical security	Survival issues, feeling threatened
2	Just below belly button	Orange	Emotion, sexuality	Isolation or feeling overloaded
3	Solar plexus	Yellow	Will, self-determination	Power struggles and control issues
4	Heart area	Green	Love, relationships	Lack of self-love, difficult relationships
5	Throat	Blue	Communication, expression	Inability to express oneself or listen
6	Between and just above eyes	Indigo	Intuition, imagi-nation	Lack of vision or imagination
7	Crown of head	Violet	Awareness, spiri-tuality	No connection to higher self
8	18" above the head	White	Receptivity to nonphysical information	Inability to hear guidance or sense outside energy

By breathing into each center in succession, using the power of intention, you can rebalance the chakras. One technique is to first connect to your *ground* and draw earth energy up through the bottoms of your feet into your legs. Imagine the energy coursing up your spine, nourishing the bones, muscles, and all the various systems, until it pours out the top of your head, fountaining back to earth, carrying with it all blocks or impurities it might have encountered on the way.

Once this flow is moving, see that same cleansing process continue as it passes over and through each energy center. As the breath moves over and through the chakras, it also nourishes and adjusts each one, creating a cycle of energy that sustains health and supports the growth of awareness.

This is a very cursory description of what can be a very powerful exercise in self-awareness. Detailed information and additional ways of working with these powerful parts of your energetic anatomy can be found in Judith's book referenced earlier, as well as Mark Rich's *Energetic Anatomy.*

Fibers

Fibers are another basic feature of the human energy-sensing system. These can be imagined as connecting strands that collect and deliver information between the outside world and your body. You may not be aware of this exchange, instead assuming that your mind or intellect is controlling the process, delivering accurate indicators of what is happening both around and within you. But mental and emotional responses do not always tell the whole picture.

By paying attention to your energetic anatomy, including your fibers, you can enhance the information that your intellect and feelings provide.

It's like a three-legged stool, resting on more than one support or channel. Including your energy anatomy in your perceptions allows for cross-checking and multiple ways of examining a situation. The first leg is your physical body, for sensing and gathering information. The second is your internal experience of mind and emotion. The third leg of the stool is the human energetic system and the component called fibers.

When you reach out to pick up a pen, you are directing your attention first, and then your hand responds. In that simple operation you have attached a fiber of attention from yourself to an object and then acted on it directly. At this level it's an automatic feature of how you function in the day-to-day world, but if you look deeper, you'll see other applications of your fibers.

In all of the detailed and layered activities you do—driving a car or playing the violin—you are directing your fibers. You could say that the fibers are the servants of your will, which is the driving force behind their activities. Your attention, will, and fibers are

tools that connect you to the environment, to objects, and also people. "The Law of Attraction" is a term coined and used to describe
some of ways this can work. The bottom line is awareness of how
you use your three-legged stool of body, self, and energy.

The way you chose to visualize the shape or anatomy of all of
these human systems is entirely dependent on your affinity with
any particular description. Your energy-sensing nodes, or centers,
and fibers are your tools for recognizing, owning, and adjusting
your experience of the environment. Here is my personal example.

Example: At the Museum

Museums contain a huge amount of information, as both physical data and emotional content. They can make me feel tired and
drowsy, even when I want to be alert and have willingly put myself
in the situation. Sometimes it's about the sheer age of an item; at
other times, it may be an issue related to what the item was used for.
Paintings viewed and venerated by many people hold a particular
depth of information, not to mention the experience of the artist.

The first time I saw the work of artist Frida Kahlo, I did not
know that she had suffered a crippling back injury. That drowsy
and exhausted museum sensation began right away, but I didn't
associate it with the energetic content in front of me. After twenty
minutes of standing before her paintings, I found myself curled up
in a ball on a bench wondering why I suddenly hurt so much. Even
though I was worried about having somehow slipped a disc, it just
didn't feel like the pain was *mine.*

And it wasn't! Because I had the skill set of using my energetic anatomy, I could recognize that the sudden sensations were
"off" somehow. My energetic structures, as described above, were
plugged directly into the environment around me. I had overloaded
my own body with information from the art, which included the
pain that Kahlo lived with as she painted. How did this happen?

Using my fibers to reach into the artwork, I had invited the content into my system via my energy centers. First I had to realize that the pain sensations were not mine, that they were being generated by outside information. Then it became possible to separate myself, to clear the data from my system, and realign myself to my own core. Core is one of the bedrock concepts of cultivating awareness. Developing this kind of discernment is the goal of the following section.

By understanding and tuning your own human energy anatomy, you can recognize and manage how places like museums and grocery stores affect you.

Your Basics: Three Steps to Radical Awareness— Ground, Core, and Edges

Cultures, religions, and spiritual practices around the world have developed ritual methods to bring awareness into the body, and most people will resonate to different techniques. Each practice has a particular feel and emphasis. The adventure is discovering what works for your individual system. Many of the techniques I'm about to describe come from the work of Lynda Caesara, a teacher of personal energy awareness. She has crafted her own methods from the work of many disciplines and teachers. The common ground is a desire to help people wake up and function in the world as it is, with grace, compassion, and confidence. My descriptions are intended to focus the knowledge on *being at home* and are a limited picture of their true power.

Ground

Grounding is often the first step in any energetic practice. Without it, you may either get lost in your mind or be swept away by circumstances around you. One of the most obvious signs that you are not grounded is a feeling of irritation or of being "short circuited."

By practicing this technique, you can learn to recognize the cues from your own body.

EXERCISE
Establishing Your Ground

Either sitting or standing, plant your feet on a surface of some sort—even if it is the floor of an airplane. Focus attention on the bottoms of your feet, feeling the bones within your feet and how they connect your skeleton to the support beneath them. Follow the bones up your legs and locate the base of your spine in your mind's eye. Settle here for a few moments, feeling the entire structure of the skeleton, holding the image of bones beneath the flesh and muscles, your skull sitting on the top of your spine.

Now, connect this entire system to the earth below you by visualizing a connecting substance, like a root system, a cord, a strong fiber, or a dense shaft of light. This connecting element originates from the base of your spine and the bottoms of your feet. Send this connecting root deep into the earth below you, straight through any intervening matter—buildings, floors, cars in motion; they do not matter. The point is to take hold of the ground and know that you have a solid connection.

Once you feel this mooring to the planet, draw its powerful presence up into your body, filling your feet, legs, torso, chest, neck, arms, hands, and head. This flow of nourishing warmth supports and feeds every cell in your body. Imagine a cup or chalice in the center of your heart area. The earth's grounding energy fills it and overflows, pouring throughout your body and out into the space surrounding you. The more you draw on earth and its supportive essence, the more the cup fills and overflows, which allows you to ground not only yourself, but also other people and the environment you stand in.

This is not a depletion of your system, because the fountain of grounding force is coming from your overflow, the excess of your connection to the earth. In fact, when you allow this well to nourish your space, it actually increases the flow and sustains and enriches your own being even more. You can choose to live here.

This flow establishes a two-way exchange system with the earth. You can pull on the huge resources of the earth to support you, and you can release or clear out unhealthy energy into the vast and powerful processing system that is the planet itself. One especially useful application of this is fixing your attention on the road beneath a moving car. As a passenger in a fast car on a curvy road, my mild discomfort was instantly eased by grounding solidly to the road itself as it hugged the terrain of the hills all around me. Another way to increase my feeling of ground is to imagine it including the entire geographical region of the Puget Sound, rather than just the area under my feet.

Core

Your core is the essence of your individual self; it is where you return, no matter what. This is the place that tells you, "Ah, this feels just right!" or "Something is wrong; act now!" It is the source of knowing when you have found just the right words to say, or food to eat, or place to sit.

EXERCISE
Locate Your Core

Imagine that deep within your body is a channel or line along your spine. It can be visualized as a stream of light, water, mist—or it can be very solid and dense. Your core is also flexible and fluid, since it can expand and contract as you become aware of it. It is easier to feel if you are already grounded and aware of your body. Some physical activities can help your awareness of core, particularly Pilates, the Alexander Technique, and Gyrotonics. Yoga and some martial arts don't always address the core, but both are enhanced when core becomes conscious. You need to *find* it and be able to bring it into your awareness.

Sit or stand and engage your ground. Look beneath your thinking mind into your center for a stillness and presence that underlies everything, that is connected to your deepest identity. Decide what your core feels like, whether it reminds you of an object or is an evocative idea, like mist or sound. Can you feel it as part of your anatomy? Experiment with making it larger, letting it fill every cell of your body.

When I make mine larger, I imagine it filling up the spaces between my joints, packing the marrow of my bones, and even extending around my body by several feet. It might help to visualize your core getting heavier or denser. One of my favorite approaches is to see mine as glowing slightly.

When you develop the habit of checking the state of your core, you also become adept at recognizing how the environment affects you. The first step is to feel your core and recognize its messages. Some people have a hard time remembering to look here for information. Instead they look outside, to other people or institutions. Core information is also hard to hear if you're tuned to the past or to stories that your intellect depends on. Sometimes relationships and circumstances block awareness of your core. This is what happens when you stay in unhealthy places or ignore your own intuition.

The first time I looked for my core, I was surprised to get an image in my mind's eye of a very large piece of kelp. Growing up in the maritime Northwest, a fisherman's daughter, I have some experience of kelp. This particular kind of kelp is rooted in the seabed, but extends up toward the water's surface in a long sinuous rope of dense material with fronds of light-receiving leaves and bulbs at the top. It is both flexible and solid, holds on tight to the earth, and moves with the tides. This works as an image for locating my own core.

I can also imagine that it's an energetic substance that expands and contracts at my command. The more vivid and intimate this becomes, the more I can realize when my core is missing. Here is the moment of choice and power; I can decide to get it back!

Loss of core may feel like simple confusion or a sense that something is off-balance. Some people experience it as losing touch with their own priorities or values. Becoming aware of your core, you can realign to your essential and highest integrity.

Edge

Skin is only one of your boundaries. Emotional boundaries are another, and most people have a fairly fine-tuned sense of when those lines get crossed or threatened. A violation of an emotional boundary can take a while to notice, however, as they often get filtered through the intellect.

Someone demands that you make them important, for example, with no respect for your own situation or feelings. You may respond by meeting this demand, or you may try to rationalize a way around it—all without seeing that it's an inappropriate request. Your boundary has been crossed, and it might result in immediate recognition, or your emotions may take a while to register in your body. In the example above, it might take a clenched jaw or a period of confused thinking to realize you have been pushed too far.

Awareness of your energetic anatomy includes another level of sensitivity: the body's energetic edge. It's the early warning system for information of all kinds, including emotional boundary violations. Knowing how to control your energetic edge is a key skill for negotiating life in a body.

You can visualize your boundary as the edge of a field or bubble that surrounds you. It can be just next to your skin, but more often it has a set point a bit further away—from a couple inches to a foot or more. This set point can move and respond to your surroundings, creating more or less of a buffer between you and the external world. Some disciplines define this field as the aura, and there are those who claim to actually see these boundaries around people.

Skill with your edge can become a powerful tool for interacting with people and for understanding the effect they may have on you. Skilled energy healers are able to read your field for information about your health, as it reflects your body, mind, emotions, and the energetic system.

Even if you never see a glowing field or aura with your own eyes, you're probably still aware of certain people or things that attract or repel you. They may have a shiny or fuzzy or slippery aspect. These words are reflections of our actual ability to sense the information in the field. Since I get the data other ways, I have let go of trying to physically see it, but I do believe that you can learn to perceive it. To that end, I heartily recommend Rich's book and the work of Barbara Ann Brennan, *Light Emerging*, for their clear and explicit exercises and illustrations.

EXERCISE
Negotiating Edges

Stand in a relaxed but grounded posture and feel into your core. See in your mind's eye the substance of your core filling your body, saturating every cell, filling the marrow of your bones, and expanding until it coats your skin evenly in your own authentic presence. Next imagine the boundary around your body, the edge of your energetic field. Even if you can't decide exactly where it is, you can imagine that your core is expanding to fill that space. By taking up all the room, your field is filled only with *your* core and nothing else.

> Hold an intention that this membrane be an effective con-
> tainer—one that serves to keep out what does not belong in
> your field, but that will let in information or energy that serves
> you. Remember that your edge is also behind you! Stand still
> and feel the size and placement of your edge. When you feel
> it clearly, try approaching objects or people and see if you
> can tell when you are getting so close there is some overlap
> or intrusion between your edge and that of another person.

Your basic skill set needs to include recognizing the boundary around yourself and what you allow to cross it. Things you encounter will trigger your own issues, emotions, or reactions; but it's also possible to register information that belongs to an object or someone else. As you continue developing the use of your energy-sensing anatomy, this will become a crucial and powerful discernment.

My adventure with the art museum is a testimony to what can happen when you do not stay aware of what you are taking in. While enjoying the paintings, I also let in powerful data about the artist and lost track of my own boundary. Ideally I could have "read" that same information about her pain but not taken it into my system and confused it with my own.

If you allow the energy of other people or things in your environment to cross your edges, your own system can become unstable. If you are not aware of this happening, it becomes harder to maintain your own core and make good decisions. It can also just feel very uncomfortable.

Whether it feels good, bad, or indifferent, the energy of other people doesn't belong inside your boundary edges. And skill with your edge means that you don't project yours where it doesn't belong. With time, it is possible to recognize the many ways that people interact, both skillfully and not so skillfully. Recognizing what is yours and what is not becomes easier when you have a clearly defined edge.

Throughout the rest of this book, I'll be referring to your *basics,* another term from Lynda Caesara. In this context, I'll be using it to point you back to ground, core, and edges. They are the tools you'll use to explore each of the nested homes. You've started with your own body, and how that defines the self. From here it's time to examine your home environment, nature, and finally the wider world.

In your own space, you can now begin to use your body's energy centers and fibers to "read" the environment, which will help you understand why it feels the way it does. With your ground, core, and edges, you place yourself into a conscious relationship with that information. So how can you make that place into the safe haven of *home?* Homemaking is more than a tidy bedroom or a full pantry; it's the ability to engage with the qualities of the space around you. Now that you're in the building, let's make it home.

Chapter 4

Homemaking
The Nested Layers of Home and Belongings (Basic Skills)

Dear Little House, Dear Shabby Street
Dear books and beds and food to eat
How feeble words are to express
The facets of your tenderness.

—House as a Mirror of Self: Exploring the
Deeper Meaning of Home, by Clare Cooper Marcus

Whether a space is bounded by walls, a shoreline, the skin of an airplane, or a row of seats in a movie theater, you are in charge of your experience. Knowing this is the first step toward recognizing the way a space feels and how you can best function in it. In this chapter, we'll examine ways to engage with the space around you. After you are grounded in that connection, you'll be able to explore each of the nested layers of *being home.*

Without that engagement you can't expect to have any effect on your surroundings or ability to bring them into alignment with

your goals and priorities. This is the difference between inhabiting a conscious, intentionally designed room and being in a mis-
matched, out-of-sync place that somehow just doesn't feel right.
The first is an aligned space, and the second can be described as
disconnected.

- Aligned Space: A desk that holds all the important tasks
  and projects in order. It also reflects your taste and contains
  things of beauty that make the work there pleasant.
- Disconnected Space: A desk stacked with paper that accu-
  mulates and never gets dealt with. You miss events, late
  notices start coming in, and you groan as you sit there.

Disconnected space can be adjusted only if you recognize how
it feels, which is why using the sensing mechanisms of ground,
core, and edges is so important. They tell you how the space
is affecting you. This might be a sense of having your vitality
drained, of wanting to give up in despair because there is just too
much to sort out. Your room could feel scattered and chaotic, too
hard to get a handle on. You might be feeling frazzled and irritable
on one hand and totally exhausted on the other. These distinc-
tions can be important. Later chapters will go into detail about
this process of interpreting your own body's signals. For now it
will help to get a sense of how physical changes in a room can
be made and the practical ways the room can become an aligned
space that supports you.

The Three Fundamental Qualities of an Environment: Function, Spatial Layout, and Energy

These are the doorways to a space that functions and feels both
good and right.

Function: How the Space Works

What are your personal requirements for functionality? Does a cluttered surface feel inspiring or exhausting? Either way or in between, you can decide what works for you. When a function feels right, you have a more positive relationship to all your things. Not only do you have an intimate connection to all the paper, decorations, and objects, but there's a constant dance between these objects. You can choreograph this evolving situation so that you can find the stamps, pay bills, and enjoy sitting at your desk.

However, it's not just about the stuff! This is a crucial aspect of the dance of relationship. It is about you and what matters to you. Your comfort with order and chaos reflects part of your identity. Many people think these circumstances are the result of what your parents taught you, the expectations of partners, or are a function of your income or busy schedule. While each of those influences may affect your identity, they don't need to become stories that limit you and your environment. Defining and creating your personal sense of function depends on facing your real feelings and your willingness to change. Without these, you have only your accumulated history and present circumstances. Instead, with awareness, they can become springboards for change and presence.

Example: Building Function out of Chaos

The kitchen counter has become a place for dumping the mail, purse, briefcase, backpack, keys, travel mugs, and pocket contents at the end of the day. It's a jumble of objects and information that have to be picked through. Establishing *function* here means asking what this counter is really supposed to do. Is it the best place to offload these things, or do they now make cooking difficult? How can you set things down without creating another problem? Function requires you to question what you want to accomplish and face what isn't working. Perhaps you have to set aside space on a different surface or get some containers to hold the mail, keys, and so forth. Part of function is separating the objects into categories so that you can see what you're really working with and if a strategy makes sense.

Spatial Layout: How the Space Looks

Layout defines where the desk is and how much room there is between it and the filing cabinet. It includes the selection of paint colors, art, and the tools on the desktop. You're defining this all the time, even if you're not really paying attention. The décor and room arrangements reflect who you are and what really matters at the moment. You can wake up to what you're saying to yourself and change the message.

Consider the way a typical living room is arranged. There is usually a focal point, a fireplace or a window. It used to be the TV, but more often that winds up in the family room or even a space dedicated to media. Why do many people not use their living rooms? They aren't used because they have become a placeholder for an idea that no longer matches how the occupants live. Instead of receiving guests in a formal living room, many Americans take visitors into the kitchen or some other comfortable spot to chat.

Unless a living room is *used* as a place to chat, it will not feel like the right place to do so! Families will typically eat together around a kitchen counter or family room table, rarely in a separate room at the heirloom table set with linen. Unless you create a room that responds to how you personally relax or entertain, it will become a storage room for furniture.

Example: How Layout Affects Chaos

After some consideration, you know that the kitchen counter really is the easiest place to drop off mail and objects, but it just isn't big enough. You create a space somewhere else for your large items, like the purse or backpack. Perhaps it's a lower shelf on a nearby bookshelf or a hook on the wall behind the door. Now the counter needs to hold fewer things, so you design a layout that can hold the objects you have sorted out. A dish for keys, a tray that will hold the day's mail—but wait . . . leaving a travel mug and a drugstore bag here makes no sense. The travel mug needs to be washed, and the bath products have to be put away; these are aspects of *function*.

Right here is where *function* helps you decide about *layout*. The mug goes into the kitchen sink instead, and the bag of purchases can be set aside for later delivery. But where? Thinking about *layout* might help you realize that you have other choices; you can set the bag down on a chair, leave it in the hallway to grab on your way to the bathroom, or perhaps you head there next without dropping the bag anywhere else! You can change habitual behavior to support your desire for a space that feels better.

Energy: How the Space Feels

Under the surface of function and spatial layout is a sea of personal and potent information. This is the binding connection between you and the physical room. It is here in the energetic information that you actually experience the sensation of *being home*. Energy is perceived and processed with the tools of your energetic anatomy, your energy centers, and fibers. By being able to *reference your core, find your ground, and maintain your edge*, you'll know how the content affects you.

Becoming aware of the energetic content in a space can seem overwhelming, but when you can manage your own body's energetic system, it becomes possible to impress your environment, to realign it so that it matches your requirements for the space. You can adjust the feeling in your office to match your longing for a calm, grounded feeling of concentration or your desire for an intense, juicy, and super-charged rush of inspiration.

The energy in a room is a bridge between your inner experience and the environment around you. It is a two-way street, and you may cross it from the physical side first with changes to the space that alter how it feels. By moving the desk or switching the orientation of a rug, you can radically shift the sense of balance and openness in the room. When you understand your own personal sensory system, you're also crossing the bridge.

By paying attention to your first energy center at the base of your spine, you can gauge your degree of safety and comfort. You can actually change how any environment feels, whether you move the furniture or not, by adjusting your awareness (edges) and knowing where you stand (ground). The third energy center, governing will, can support you to make changes and take charge. And finally, when you learn to read and acknowledge the information coming from the sixth and seventh energy centers, those that manage intuition, imagination, and awareness, you'll know when you have it just right.

These skills result in an exchange with your surroundings, a spacious sense of possibility and grace. You can move in your world with fluidity and confidence.

Example: Taming Chaos with Energetic Awareness

Here you are, facing the kitchen counter with an armload of stuff. You're finally home, and all these things need to be dealt with, but already the prospect makes you want to throw it all on the floor and lie down. Where are your ground and core right now? Probably nowhere in sight, so first slow down and find them.

Once you're aware of where you stand, you'll remember the hook for your purse or backpack. With more clarity about function, you can remember where to put the keys so you'll find them later—they are a part of your support system and deserve a home that you can trust. You can make the act of placing the mail on the counter into a statement about your priorities and intentions. Awareness becomes your gateway to *being home.*

More Ways of Being Home

The three fundamental concepts can support you in any setting. In these examples you'll see how function, spatial layout, and energy all play a part in negotiating your relationship with an environment.

To recap:

- Function tells you the way it works, its practical use.
- Layout is the way it looks, where everything is.
- Energy is the way it feels, giving you information about how the space affects you.

Designing a Personal Office: Getting Things Done

What happens in your personal office? Paper is stored, you write with a favorite pen, you pay bills, and you probably use a computer, a phone, and a printer. *Function* here consists of systems for dealing with information and getting tasks done. Your particular kind of information or work will dictate the way *function* supports you, whether you prefer a filing cabinet or open shelves, a desk or a drafting board, a computer or an easel. A key feature of *function* in this case can directly connect you to your first home—your body.

Ergonomics is the applied science of designing equipment and furniture to reduce the fatigue and discomfort of the user. By including awareness of ergonomics in your workspace, you support both what you do there and the body you live in. In doing so, you manage to come home even as you work!

No matter what the room looks like or how big it is, you'll need to be clear about what these tools are, which ones are essential, and which might be extras. If you'd like to add an easy chair and lamp for reading, consider whether it's a requirement or just a nice idea. Your clarity about the priority of things will determine the next step.

Spatial layout will determine the placement of all the pieces you just defined. Are you in a spare bedroom with plenty of light or making do with a corner of the family room in the basement? You may realize that *function* has to be created some other way if your tools don't fit the space. Consider the fixed qualities first, natural light or lack of it, other uses that the room has to support (Is the closet full of things that could be moved to the basement?), and how you want to move around in it. Your orientation as you sit or stand to work and the ease of reaching tools will determine how you place furniture and decorations.

This part of the process can get stuck if you're not willing to experiment. Moving furniture and heavy objects may seem like far too much trouble, but these changes in the way a space feels can be amazing. By rotating a throw rug by ninety degrees you can completely reorient the directional sense in a very small room. These shifts of angle or placement can also fine-tune your sense of the flow of energy, making the room more inviting and attractive.

Energy has been a factor all along as you've been making decisions and considering your options. At each step, you consult your own human energy sensing system, measuring how the choices and changes feel. Sometimes thinking about the process from a rational or logical standpoint doesn't quite work or provide enough feedback. Spatial decisions do not come naturally to everyone, and if you find yourself getting confused or frustrated, it can help to stop and listen to the energetic sensing system you are born with: your ground, core, and edges. The information you receive with these tools can help you recognize what should change.

The whole process might look like this: After working in a hallway niche on a tiny table, you finally have a real desk in the guest room and need to rearrange your files and supplies. Thanks to having wide, shallow drawers, the desk now holds all the small tools right at your fingertips. But since it is a library-style table, there are no deep file drawers, and it's time to replace a nasty, old, creaking metal file cabinet. A lateral file cabinet will not only fit nicely next to the desk, but also provide a surface for the printer, making even more desktop real estate available for projects and sorting paper.

Function has now defined the shape of the work space; you can reach the files, know where the stapler lives, and decide exactly how many tools to place at your fingertips.

Layout begins here, with choices about those locations and the arrangement of photographs and art objects you'll enjoy seeing on the wall and windowsill.

Using your *energetic* senses, you feel the sense of belonging in your core as you work, because you've placed meaningful objects right here: a basket reminiscent of travels and some beautiful hand-bound books that delight the eye with their textures of paper and fabric. The simple utilitarian objects also speak with an energetic voice that demands your attention. Rusty scissors tell you about all three aspects—function, layout, and energy—all saying: *Replace this tool!*

Setting Up Home with Another Person: Sharing Territory

The decision to move in with someone is a choice to share life on a whole new level. Usually *function* is the first consideration. Where will you live: a home already occupied by one of you or a new place? Your decisions will rest on negotiating your requirements for location and your hopes for how the space will work. Remember that there is an energetic quality to these choices about function. This is important to keep in mind when two people are facing the effort needed to make adjustments and compromises.

For a fortunate pair, these issues may solve themselves with no problems, and sometimes it will be obvious who and what will move or stay. Focusing on practical issues of function can help you decide how to share the priorities for space to accommodate children, pets, or work.

Layout can be either the fun part or the most daunting challenge of sharing space with another person. Furniture, decorations, and the details of how rooms are laid out will all need to be talked about, and this can be stressful if one of you resists change. Be prepared for all sorts of information to be revealed: assumptions that may not have been consciously faced, places of habit and tradition that need to be first acknowledged and possibly honored—even if you disagree.

These adjustments might be as minor as where you keep the sugar or as value laden as keeping a family piano. On the other hand, you could be surprised at what matters to the other person. He or she may not care about the piano, but put their foot down about the sugar location. Setting up a household with someone requires honest communication, whether they are a partner, a friend, or someone you barely know. Until you actually talk about the real meaning of any decision, you won't be able to negotiate a solution, find out that he cherishes the piano, or understand that having the sugar on the table reminds her of a beloved grandma. In a later chapter, I'll introduce a process for mutual satisfaction with these decisions.

Again, the *energetic* information you're dancing with while combining households is entwined in both the functional use and the layout. But here you're also following the steps of another person, taking turns recognizing where each of you wants to go and how it feels when you lead or follow.

Here is an example of this from my own experience that may seem like a simple layout issue, but involved a reading of how a space was composed. My sweetheart and I decided to rearrange the decorations around the fireplace mantel and hearth. I replaced some candles and moved several decorations, a porcelain bowl, and a pair of hand-blown glass goblets on the upper surface. He in turn moved a hip-tall ceramic pot to one side of the hearth. This left a large, carved-wood African antelope in an awkward location on the other side.

We had been playing with both *function* and *layout* up to this point, and now moved into the *energetic* side of the process. We must have sat and looked at this arrangement for ten minutes, both dissatisfied with the feel of the composition. Suddenly he got up and turned the antelope to face the opposite direction. It is an asymmetrical beast, and once it was rotated, the shape fit the wall space perfectly.

Embedded in this process is the use of our fourth and fifth energy centers. Aware of our relationship, we could trust that our silent contemplation of the design was a connection in itself (the fourth energy center is also known as the heart chakra). Once the antelope had been moved, we could express our reactions via a healthy use of the fifth center, also called the throat chakra, which governs accurate and appropriate expression.

With willingness to experiment and trust these subjective cues, you can make profound changes to the layout and functional use in your world. Such a tiny change and that whole end of the room fell into place with a resounding click of satisfaction.

A Preview: Moving outside Your Home into the Wider World

Shopping in an unfamiliar grocery store is a great opportunity to practice environmental awareness skills; it's a place that's full of data, potential chaos, and practical results. This might seem simplistic, but mundane and repetitive experiences can be the most powerful doorways to new awareness. The questions and concerns listed below for each of the fundamental qualities may seem automatic and not worth the time it takes to ask them, but they illustrate the depth of information available in every space you occupy. And the breakdown between function, layout, and energy will depend upon how *you* see them as tools for beginning to recognize the content all around you.

You are *already* using the skill set everywhere, and by making it conscious, you gain even more ease and comfort in the places that are not as easy or familiar. Finding *function* out in the world takes you to a new series of challenges. The reality is that you are dealing with situations that may not be easy or adjustable. Now you're dancing with a turnstile or a traffic light instead of a more malleable partner, like your own desk. The key is to understand your options and gather accurate information for your decisions.

A new situation can bring up a mixed cocktail of emotions, ranging from mild curiosity to total panic. Every experience of an environment depends on your ability to track where you are and what that environment is saying to you.

Function: How use is supported at the grocery store.

- Did I remember to bring my own bag, or will I have to buy one?
- Where are the shopping carts or baskets, and which size do I need?

Layout: How spatial locations are related.

- How narrow are the aisles; are the displays in the way, or are they interesting?
- Where is the signage; is it easily seen, overhead, or on the sides?

Energy: What the feeling of the place says.

- Are my encounters with the people competitive or companionable?
- Am I relaxed and comfortable or unaccountably irritated by being here?

The first order of business for me when shopping in the urban grocery store, rather than my familiar neighborhood market, was navigating the *function* of a crowded entryway that was full of shoppers on their way out. The space itself was too tight for anyone to stand around long; people had to keep moving and create room for one another. Locating a shopping cart or basket became a game of dodgeball, an issue of non-*function* and a confusing *layout*.

Once beyond the entrance, the aisles opened up to a more spacious plan, and the islands of specials and sale items actually served as little rest stops or accents in the broad passages. *Function* was reflected in a system of numbered tickets for the deli counter, and the *layout* provided people waiting their turn a place to stand without blocking either the counter or the ticket machine. It felt obvious and simple; I didn't have to wonder how to get help, even in the crowd.

I noticed clear signage, making it easy to figure out where the crushed ice was. This is something I like to pick up last, and the *layout* made it easy to find, but it was placed at an awkward location at the back of the store, far away from the checkout stands. While I appreciated the information in the *functioning* of the store, I didn't like the *layout* of it. Having the knowledge made it easier to use the space, whether I liked it or not.

Within the busy movement all around me, I could see the *energetic* information about how to behave in concert with people negotiating aisles and each other. The classic situation of using this awareness is—you guessed it—at the checkout stand.

There I stood with about five options to choose from, each one holding different people, potential interactions, and time expenditures. And I knew from experience that if my goal was minimal time, the discernment was not going to be a logical one. It would be based on past experience and judgments that had little to do with this line, these people, or the contents of their baskets. Even the automated checkout stations are fraught with data. Are the people in front of me having an easy time of it? Do I even know how to use them, or am I willing to learn on the fly? How do I choose?

I look first at who is standing in the short lines. If they are people I'd like to stand behind, people who seem competent, awake, focused on the process of unloading and paying, that's where I stand. But perhaps it's a day with plenty of time, and I'd rather wait my turn with the young mother who is wrestling a toddler; perhaps I am in the mood to make silly faces and engage the child.

Without awareness of my own reactions, I can't accurately choose my options. Even if I think I'm relaxed enough to wait behind the mother with the overloaded cart, if I don't recognize that she may also take much longer to locate her wallet, I'll quickly question my own judgment. Hmmm, she looks a bit preoccupied and irritable. Am I grounded enough to stay relaxed if she turns and snarls at me for grinning at her child? Maybe I'll stay out of her way and brave the automatic checkout stations this time.

There are ways to practice these kinds of choices. Using energetic senses requires me to have my own system functioning, so the first order of business is to check my ground, core, and edges. Ideally, these are always in place as a baseline, but being human, if a particular challenge arises, I double check that I'm really operating from a stable place. Take another look at the exercises in chapter 3 before doing the next one. Having your basics in place will enable you to measure the differences between kinds of environments and make better choices as you navigate them.

EXERCISE
Compare Two Places

Consider two places where you have spent some considerable amount of time. Pick one that feels positive—right, balanced, or just pleasing to your senses. I suggest you write about your reactions to create an anchor with that experience. Now pick another that is negative—constricted, irritating, or unpleasant. You can go back in time to one that is particularly powerful, but do select a pair that are very different—perhaps your grandmother's kitchen as you remember it and a conference room where you routinely attend meetings. Either of these examples might be positive or negative!

Using the three fundamental qualities—*function, layout,* and *energy*—look at how these two different places affect you as you place yourself in them. Which of the qualities matters most? Perhaps the *function* is so chaotic it's hard to notice any *layout,* and this sets up a constricted feeling that sends you out of the room. Perhaps the people in the room override the functional layout, and it's hard to pay attention. Can you imagine ways to adjust the functionality or layout? If not, can paying attention to these qualities change how you understand your experience?

Once you've examined how you experience two very different kinds of places, return to a strong sense of your energetic anatomy; reground, locate your core and edges. Does this give you more options? There may be nothing you can do to take charge of chaotic space or adjust the human interactions going on in it. Even so, being at home in your own body will make it easier to stay aware and choose a response. In an upsetting encounter in a family kitchen, perhaps it's easier to just wash the dishes in silence; in a tense conference room, maybe you can pick a seat near a supportive person.

Conclusion

Making yourself at home in the world and your own living space requires awareness of your intentions, as well as what exists outside and all around you. The fundamental qualities of that outer space, whether it's your quiet, morning kitchen or a crowded deli counter, are the tools and measuring sticks for change. In chapter 5, you'll start to play with more details of the third nested layer: home and belongings.

For now, it's time to kick off your shoes and settle in . . . after you carefully consider where those shoes just landed.

Chapter 5

Settling In
Being Connected to Place

> If you stuff things under your bed, they still have energy
> and are calling out to you. You may as well put them
> under the covers with you.
>
> —*Clutter Busting: Letting Go of*
> *What's Holding You Back,* by Brooks Palmer

How the Physical Is Linked to Mind and Feelings

The paraphrase above from a great organizing book by Brooks
Palmer, *Clutter Busting,* reminds me of an insight from the world of
feng shui. You can suffer energetic distress in a pristine, tidy space
if the hidden spaces—basements, closets, and drawers—are full of
unacknowledged things: decisions, history, or stories. Much more,
when your rooms feel chaotic or hard to use, you pay a price in
both realms: the physical and the energetic.

The things you surround yourself with represent a deep mix
of messages. How has an object come to "belong" to you, and
did you actually choose to acquire it? For many people, anything

that currently exists in their homes not only belongs to them, but somehow develops a personality or value that the owner is now responsible for protecting. This is a serious inversion of worth, as you and your space are what matters, and you should give meaning to the objects around you with awareness, not by default. This is a radical concept to many people living with clutter. Having something does not mean you need to keep it.

A depression-era family member's memory, the ethical code of keeping and reusing, plans to make use of things later—these are stories that hold you in a pattern of being owned by possessions. Reasons for keeping things range from a rational desire to be ecologically responsible to deep-seated fears about being a bad person if you allow a broken object to end up in a landfill. Some of these reasons, once recognized, are easy to dismiss; others may take some thought about your real desire to make lasting changes in a cluttered environment.

A Spectrum of Attachment

Attachment to objects is a very wide spectrum, and while everyone has some degree of ownership, there are people at the far end with more serious issues at stake. These are people unwilling to throw away a broken and truly useless object; rather than contribute to landfill, they live in one. It may require work with a therapist or a willingness to dig deeper, especially if throwing away such things feels like cutting off a limb. This common reaction among hoarders is best addressed by a specialist who knows the complexities of this disorder. The intense feelings that go along with hoarding have to be faced, and the solution is never a case of simple willpower or tidiness.

Here is an example of how things are connected through mind and feelings from an average closet in the middle of the attachment spectrum. Clothing is a personal and powerful statement about who we are and how we want to be seen. It can be both a pleasure and a trial. When I left my career in architecture, I had lots of expensive skirts that required dry-cleaning. Many stories were attached to these items: *I am a professional; I spent hard-earned money to buy and keep these clothes; they still fit; I might wear them somewhere else; they are too "good" to donate; I might "need" them later.* And so on.

As I moved more deeply into my work as an organizer, my closet began to fill with comfortable pants and shirts that let me crawl around on other people's closet floors. Soon, there was really no room for the skirts, and I had to face the fact that my days as a skirt-wearing architect were over. Ouch!! Were they clutter? Not by many standards. *But by the standards of the life I had chosen, they had become clutter.*

The process of letting go of objects is not about the actual thing. Your relationship to the thing defines both it *and you.* It is a matter of your very identity. In order to create the sense of being home, your physical space and the clothes that define you must be conscious choices. It should not be filled with stuff that exists for a lot of old reasons.

Daniel J. Siegel writes in his book *Mindsight* that by becoming aware of our internal mental world, we can actually change the landscape of our thinking, which can "free us from patterns of mind that are getting in the way of living our lives to the fullest." The challenge for me was to recognize that I was hanging on to an identity with skirts, while my actual closet proved that they didn't work for me anymore. Once my thinking landscape included that reality, it became much easier to put the skirts into the donate box. The landscape of my closet became spacious and easy to use, full of what I enjoy wearing.

Dealing with clutter and becoming organized covers a broad range of situations. Whether you just don't like filing, or find yourself living in mild but general chaos, or suffer from more severe hoarding issues, keep in mind that creating order is always about awareness of your relationship with things and the space around you. No matter where you are in that range, you can begin to fine-tune this connection between stuff and your experience.

Your Energetic Connection between Outside and Inside

The energy you feel in a room is, in fact, a bridge between your inner experience and the environment around you. As mentioned earlier, it's a two-way street, and you can make changes coming from either side: the internal feelings or the external moving of furniture or paper. This bridge ties the actual stuff scattered all over the countertops with your inner world of thoughts and feelings. This is not mystical or intangible, it's real; clutter affects your experience, and when you become aware of this connection, you can adjust your spaces with skill and deep satisfaction. Awareness of energy makes it possible to fine-tune and improve the balance between your inner and outer worlds.

If you are comfortable with guided visualizations, the following exercise is a way to experience this bridge as a tree, an organic expression of healthy connection to environment. If not, feel free to read it as a metaphor for the idea of this link.

EXERCISE
The Tree

How is the physical linked to your inner world? A tree stands on the earth and also reaches into the sky. The roots are deeply buried in the ground, drawing nutrients, water, and support. At the same time, the leaves and flowers exist above in the open air, processing sunlight, attracting pollinators, and connecting the tree to the environment at the other end.

Imagine yourself as a tree, one that is part of a forest. Your roots, deeply embedded in the earth, represent your past, family history, belief systems, and values, including unconscious patterns of behavior. You depend on these roots to hold you up; they provide reasons for your actions and choices. The root system holds the mental and emotional issues that support the trunk and upper branches and leaves. If they are unhealthy, the whole organism suffers.

The tree trunk is your body; it's what connects your root identity and the upper leafy parts that are up in the air, exposed to weather and circumstances. These leaves and flowers receive information and ideas and otherwise relate to the outside world. You are nurtured equally from both ends, the roots of your inner being and your relationship to the larger world of the forest surrounding you.

The tree as a whole organism represents your body's energetic anatomy. Using the information provided by your roots, the trunk connects you by *being grounded, having a strong core, and having clear edges.* These are the tools we explored in chapter 3. They connect the trunk to the leaves and branches. These leaves and branches process light, air, temperature, and environmental conditions. In your energetic anatomy, they also reach for inspiration and connection.

In a healthy tree, the roots serve the whole organism (positive conscious internal messages), and the trunk provides the link (physical awareness and ease in the body) to efficient and creative interaction with the world. The physical objects you choose to live with are the fruit of your tree. Decorations, clothes, tools, and paper are all products of this particular tree and its place in the forest. They illustrate how your inner world is manifested in the environment.

An Inside Job: The Emotional and Mental Work of Clutter Clearing

It would be easy to digress into the details of organizing and techniques for clearing clutter, but this book is about the process of conscious homecoming. In the bibliography, you'll find my practical favorites by Julie Morgenstern, Peter Walsh, and Brooks Palmer, among others. These writers have already provided clear and valuable steps for creating balance in your environment. Settling in requires addressing this side of the equation.

By dealing with clutter, you begin to link your surroundings and your internal, subjective experience. Even if you have zero clutter, your body's energetic anatomy and awareness connect your environment to the feeling of being at home. Whether your roots predispose you to clutter or not, whether your leaves and branches are distracted and unfocused or tidy and well trimmed, you can bring this tree into a pleasing shape in whose shade you'll find home.

Clutter is not limited to physical objects. It can show up in your experience as mental, emotional, or spiritual distraction and unease. In some cases, dealing with the physical side will open the door to facing the internal chaos. In your personal equation, this may be the way to start. The important thing to remember is that external and internal are a linked whole, a feature of the organism that you are. Changes to any part will affect that whole.

One way to start is to acknowledge the underlying emotions and stories that you tell yourself about clutter. There is a single key question to ask about any object you live with.

Does this item support or drain me? Pay attention to your first response. Refer to the tree again and ask if your root system feels nurtured by this thing. Does it remind you of what really matters? There is a surefire way of knowing that your answer is authentic.

Ask another person to show you the object in question when you're not expecting it. All they have to do is hold it up or, if it's large, point to it and say, "How about this?" If something supports you, your expression will show it.

An object reflects the relationship you have with it.

Your face has shown without a doubt that the object supports you at an internal level. The next question to ask is: Does the item have a "home"? This may not be as easy as it sounds, but the effort to establish a place for it will be justified by the look of delight on your face later.

If the object drains you, your face will also express that reaction.

You can trust that immediate feeling of dismay or discomfort.

Keeping it drains not just your closet space, but your emotional and mental state. What makes this item worth the real estate it takes up in your limited physical space? Any stories you come up with will be justifications and reasons that are sabotaging your well-being. The only question you should be asking now is: how shall I get rid of it?

Your facial reaction might also be neutral, and that just means the item can be judged on its own merits. Is it useful or not? Be aware that even a "neutral" item can trigger a backstory, a chain of reasons for keeping it that do not really support you. A truly neutral object will not need you to justify its existence in your closet.

REMINDER: Just like a room, an object has the three qualities of *function, layout, and energy.* Sometimes it's difficult to focus on *why* the thing doesn't have a home, even if it seems to meet the criterion on energetically supporting you. This may point back to questions of *function* (how the object works for you) or *layout* (its relationship to other things). By bringing your attention to these questions, you can begin to take responsibility for all your stuff, reducing the amount that you now recognize as clutter.

How do you deal with what drains you? Even with the shadow of that drained look on your face, you may be coming up with reasons for keeping the object. The story I hear most often is some version of "because I have it."

I submit that this is not good enough. Objects can lose value over time, become like wallpaper, and move from the delight category to the neutral or even start to drain you. It honors neither yourself nor the object to hang onto it, especially if you know that a particular yellow sweater is a bad color for your skin tone or that the cuffs will never cover your wrists again. Every time you put that sweater on, you are saying, *I value this object more than my own real opinion of it.*

It's time to face the relationship you have with the sweater *now;* let it go and move on. Set that sweater free! Once you've made this choice, don't hesitate. You may get hung up on how to let go, believing you're responsible for the *well-being of the object.* It must be appreciated by someone you know or go to a special new home. Another avoidance strategy is only letting go if it earns you some money. Garage sales tend to generate more stress than income, unless you actually enjoy the process for itself.

These are stories that can derail the momentum of change. They are messages from your root system about worth and value and rightness. If it's easy for you to meet such criteria, then there's no problem, but if these messages result in being stuck or paralyzed, they need to be questioned. Are they really in your best interest? Once you know that an object is a drain, let go of it quickly. This creates space for what does feel right. You are learning to recognize the energetic component of objects, and knowing that something can make you feel heavy, tired, or frustrated is a big step toward recognizing clutter for what it is—a draining away of what matters.

Some stories are about being a certain kind of person and have nothing to do with the value of the object. They are each a way of telling yourself that you made a good decision to get this item, it was a deal, and you didn't waste your money, and so on.

Confusing *Having* with *Being*

Actual value is in the use and emotional message of an object. The problem happens when these get confused with your need to be a "good, thrifty, or responsible person." You can respond to and honor the emotional message of an object without believing that it determines who you are. You can even appreciate things without having or keeping them.

The crux of the matter is awareness of those stories and the ability to recognize the impact of the stuff on your environment. Will you really use it? Is there a place to put it? Will it be a positive addition to your space? Can you really afford it? If the answers are yes, then your stories are probably not getting you in trouble. But if you are driven by stories to bring home every free coffee table you see, save all containers just in case, and never donate clothing that stills fits, then it may be time to reevaluate.

- Ordinary possessions are not sacred and cannot ever make you "good."
- You, on the other hand, are sacred.
- Your things can reflect you, but they do not give you value . . . not really, ever.

Remember those skirts I had a hard time letting out the door? They were draining my ability to be present in the work I love now, getting in the way and reminding me of money spent. Instead, I now have room for comfortable clothes I enjoy wearing daily.

Some possessions do have a quality of the sacred: religious icons, family pictures, or gifts from loved ones. The key is remembering that you have imparted sanctity to that object, and it therefore has value particular to you. This aspect of an object can be shared by a group of people, but again, it is the human relationship that gives meaning.

Energetic Awareness: Settling into Being

Once you've kicked off those shoes and then decided to put them somewhere they belong, you've settled in. There's more: the process of being at home goes beyond the physical clutter issues and includes the energetic awareness of your active and vital relationship to the rooms and things around you.

The quality of energy in our homes is especially important; this is where patterns are made and deepened like well-worn hollows in a set of stairs or the shiny place where our hands always brush against a cupboard. Just as you leave physical traces of your use, feelings and experiences leave a trail of information that you can learn to perceive. Becoming conscious of these cues is the key to fully owning and adjusting how your space feels and ultimately supports you.

Authority: How You Influence the World

As you step into relationship with your home, you'll recognize that awareness creates a framework for choice and action. How you move forward is a process of owning your authority. By taking responsibility for how you function in your own space, you can reinforce your self-trust. It requires honest and open acceptance of the consequences without excess guilt or avoidance. The word "responsibility" has been twisted for many people. It has come to mean "blame" instead of the ability to *respond* to all situations. At its most potent, being responsible enables you to manage both what you create and what you encounter. This liberating stance is what I mean by *Authority*.

Here is a simple and obvious example based in concrete reality: You face the piles of mail on the kitchen counter, left for weeks at a time, and own the consequence of paying a late fee on your phone bill. You have created this external event—loss of service—with your actions. When you retake authority over the mail and paying bills, the outside world will reflect your actions and—voilà!—phone service resumes.

Freedom: How You Are Affected by the World

Owning your role in how the environment feels is one side of an equation. In order for the equation to balance, you need to recognize how the world affects you. With authority over your side of the relationship, you can learn to change and consciously moderate the impact of places and settings on your body, mind, and emotions. Being able to juggle this equation—understanding the parts you can and can't control—is a process that aligns you with your surroundings.

Any situation that you allow to stagnate becomes a potential drain on your time or resources. In your environment, these pockets of stale real estate also deplete your vitality. It's like the objects under the bed that you may as well take under the covers with you at night. Remember that if those objects are neatly contained in clean labeled boxes, it's not such a terrible image; but if the bed is sitting on heaps of old papers, lost socks, and general chaos, the energetic load going to bed with you at night is wearing and unhealthy. In both of these cases, you are feeling the impact of the situation on your body, mind, and general well-being, whether you recognize it or not.

Operating in the world with an accurate gauge of how you're affected by circumstances is crucial. This helps you see that even hidden pockets of disorder can contaminate your sense of ease. Freedom is the moment you sense the weight of those objects and get them out of your sleeping space and your mind.

How Authority and Freedom Lead to Change

By addressing the concrete aspects of *function* and *layout* with authority and stepping into the freedom of self-awareness, it becomes possible to adjust the way your environment feels. This is the point at which you are engaging the *energetic content*.

When you create the experience of calm, ordered space in your bedroom, or any reflection of your personal values for that space, the room will begin to align itself to your personal energetic anatomy. Your environment can actually reference and reflect your *core*. This is the feeling of being at home.

Mastery of this alignment and the ability to make changes is rooted in attention to your energetic anatomy. It also involves starting a dialog with your surroundings. In chapter 7, you'll find a full set of guidelines for aligning your rooms in a process called *clearing*.

Example: Turning a Spare Room into a Real Room

Imagine an unused bedroom left by a departing child, or an empty recreation room in a suburban basement, or even the dining room that never entertains a meal. Pick a space that is not being used the way it's meant to be or one that never really had a purpose. This means you'll have to be honest with yourself about what's happening and recognize the reasons and excuses that hold the situation in place. Repurposing a dining room may be too much to start with, as it could be full of family furniture or things you spent "good money" on. It might involve a bigger step, possibly some negotiation with other people, to turn that dining room into a place dedicated to stamps, quilting, or fly-fishing.

But the "spare" bedroom, the place that is full of clothes no one wears, books no one reads, or is the dumping ground for anything that doesn't have a home—this is a prime candidate for reclamation. How does this room affect you now? In years of professional organizing, I have carefully watched my clients enter such rooms. What I see in them most often is a combination of being dismayed and overwhelmed, tinged with self-recrimination and the desire to run the other direction as fast as possible.

Once you acknowledge the impact this room has on your body, mind, and emotions, the dance can begin. Even if you know that the abandoned or ignored space drains your vitality and triggers feelings of guilt or frustration, it's common to pretend that it's not really happening or dismiss it as an isolated problem. It's not isolated, and it can permeate the rest of the house!

Taking stock and moving ahead with the physical changes will start the process of deep change. Suppose the goal is to create a separate room for reading, drawing, and journaling. Does this space really require a bed? If not, do you really want your special room to be handicapped by furniture that's used only three times a year? Perhaps you get an inflatable bed instead.

If you can open your mind to other possibilities, the room itself will open up to you and your dream for it. By daring to go through all the forgotten objects and find them appropriate homes (perhaps not in yours!), your relationship with the no-longer-spare room can develop. You have stepped into *authority* and *freedom* by *aligning* the environment with yourself. It's just the beginning.

This next exercise is adapted from several techniques in *An Unused Intelligence,* by Andy Bryner and Dawna Markova, and *The Unfolding Now: Realizing Your True Nature through the Practice of Presence,* by A. H. Almaas. The purpose is to expand your ability to read the information all around you and its effect on you. Beyond reading the feeling of your surroundings, you'll become adept at understanding why some places feel right *to you* and others do not. These are prerequisite skills for adjusting and managing your experience at home and anywhere you go.

EXERCISES
Reading Personal Clues
in the Environment

1. Awareness

Is this place a *Yes* or a *No?* Begin with your own body and energetic anatomy. Settle somewhere comfortable and be still for five minutes with your basics in place: awareness of your *ground, core, and edges,* including the *field* around your body. Then call to mind some real locations that bring up strong sensory responses for you. Select some that are positive, a *Yes* feeling, and at least one that is a definite *No.* Write a list of the physical and emotional feelings associated with each type of place, but avoid falling into stories or drama about the past.

Examples:

- A beach park = tingling vitality, openness, a larger perspective. These could be *Yes* cues, conveying that your body, mind, and feelings are in a place of beauty, interest, or pleasure.

- Stuck in traffic = tight jaw and shoulders, demanding thoughts, and irritability. These might be your personal *No* signals, messages that something is not right.

- Eating breakfast in your kitchen = relaxed, informal, feeling supported by familiar things. Again, these are probably *Yes* cues that you belong and are safe, able to manage the day ahead.

Only you can determine the meaning of these cues. For some people, the sense of expansive openness at the beach could feel threatening. For others, the tight jaw of the traffic example might be a sign of concentration. *Yes and No are subjective, not fixed.*

Once you become receptive to these cues, you can learn how to use them for change. Many people either overlook their subtle reactions or try to moderate them. This can look like dismissing, ignoring, justifying, or somehow translating these honest reactions into something you can control or shape into a more acceptable experience. In any case, this constitutes meddling with your own personal feedback system. If you tend to dismiss your own reactions or create stories about them, the previous examples might look like this:

- The beach is nice, but everyone likes it here, so what? It just reminds me of somewhere I went as a kid; all beaches are the same.

- This is how I always feel when I drive; there are maniacs on the road and naturally I am tense.

- The kitchen is so cozy this morning, *but . . .* I should clean the oven, wax the floor, and, oh dear, I have a meeting downtown in an hour.

The key is to become aware of what is really happening inside your body and its powerful energetic anatomy. It is receiving information from the outside and presenting you with choices and data with which to adjust your experience.

2. Authority

Now identify places in your own home that trigger your cues, both *Yes* and *No*. Consider the places you enjoy sitting down to relax, the specific chair or window that signals ease and comfort. What are the places at home that irritate or frustrate or "pinch" you—a messy desk or a cupboard that always sticks? Go and stand in these places, noting the real sensations, thoughts, and emotions. Once you can read the messages of your own body, mind, and feelings, it's possible to sort out what needs to change.

Example: Recognize the Difference

The stairway to my garage feels narrow and musty; I shrink a bit and feel impatient. It's a minor but nagging *No*. The entrance hallway is painted a deep raspberry color and every time I come in I am delighted by it and the contrast with the map on the wall; it feels warm and whimsical, a clear *Yes*. In my space, I trust these reactions.

3. Freedom

Freedom lies in the ability to act on the cues all around you, to acknowledge your part of the equation and determine what happens next, whether it is a physical alteration, an internal shift, or some combination of both. You may even discover that one leads to the other in subtle or profound ways.

Example: Choosing to Make Changes

That narrow stairway to the garage can be improved by sweeping it more often. The walls hold hanging tools, a broom, and a dustpan, all of which could be moved further down the wall, opening up the passageway. After I do these small tasks, I notice that instead of feeling constricted and irritated as I go down the steps, I am now led out into the world beyond my garage; the steps have become a transition point where my day outside home begins. That new feeling, in turn, makes it easier to take care of this neglected part of my home.

Sometimes it's easy to adjust the physical situation, but in other cases the shift needs to happen in your attitude or approach. Either way, this is the crucial step of ownership that can lead to change. It starts with you. This is where awareness and authority lead to freedom. Consider one of your own examples and explore ways of shifting the situation, either with a physical change or an adjustment of your relationship to that place. Either one may be a powerful catalyst for improvement.

By sensing and owning your reactions, you reveal an honest relationship with your surroundings. Resisting ownership of these responses not only leads to feelings of being stuck, it is a way of rejecting who you are, your very being. If you want to create a sense of home, it's important to know all about who lives there!

Beyond your home, you can read and understand the cues that exist everywhere you go. You will encounter cues that read as *yes* or *no* and many that lie in between. Your skill at recognizing them with the tool of your sensing body can be learned and improved as you practice awareness. This larger context includes other people, as well as social and cultural messages. It's the same challenge; with awareness of your relationship to all this input, you can navigate situations and places with comfort and skill.

Owning What's Mine and Knowing What Isn't

It will be helpful to develop a few more skills and make them second nature as you embark on this adventure. When you begin taking responsibility for your experience and how you affect your surroundings, it's important to know the difference between what is yours to manage and what belongs to other people. Sometimes the energetic content of a place or circumstance intrudes on you; this can happen if you're in a receptive mood and not paying attention to your edges. You might also unknowingly connect with information that is not yours to process.

Ownership skills will help you sort out the difference between your own reactions to events and places and those of other people. Once you're able to claim your honest reactions in body, mind, and emotions, it gets easier to recognize that some information you encounter is *not* yours. My encounter with the art of Frida Kahlo, described in chapter 3, is a good example of this. I had allowed the information in her paintings inside my energetic edge and wound up feeling some of the physical pain that imbued the imagery. The pain itself felt real but belonged to paintings that had in turn become the carrier of Kahlo's experience.

By developing awareness of your own energetic anatomy, you can sort out the incoming information associated with a person, a place, or an object. When you compare it to your own ground, core, and the field within your edge that is completely and purely yours, the difference will become more obvious.

Is it mine or not? People, events, and objects can affect us in many ways. Some will clearly feel like an intrusion or knock you off center in some way. Others may get across the edge of your energy anatomy into your field without you noticing. This can happen when you open up to something, like me in the museum or as you stroll through a crowded grocery store.

The next exercise will help you practice coming home to your physical body and its ability to tell you about your environment. It will clarify the *ownership* of what you encounter. It includes some techniques for clearing out information that is not yours.

EXERCISE
Ownership

Preparation: Put your *basics* in place: ground, core, and edge. In this state, you are rooted in the earth and solidly aware of the essence or marrow of your internal being. These *basics* hold and ground the space that is *yours*. Now you'll learn how to clear that space and keep track of the condition and functioning of the boundary between you and what is outside.

There are a number of ways to feel your core and the particular essence of your energetic self. It can be a vibration or frequency, like the sound of a bell, or a deep stillness. For some people, it helps to say your name and feel how it resonates in your body. Listen to sounds or notice any colors or sensations that arise as you speak your name into your bones, flesh, muscles, and marrow. For others the pure sensation of inner wholeness or consistency is enough.

Relax and look deeply with no preconceived notions about what you'll find. Thinking or worrying about what might show up will only cloud your perceptions. Let your name or other sense of *core* fill all the cells of your body, saturate your marrow, and then expand to permeate the entire space of your field.

Now scan again for anything that is resisting, feels off, or seems to pull your attention to a particular place within your field. If this place or sensation does not match the feeling of your core or spoken name, *it is not yours.* You may or may not know what it is or where it came from; the main task is to remove it from your body, so try not to get distracted by needing a story about it. As you gain skill with *ownership,* you'll begin to recognize more information about what you've held or let into your energetic anatomy, but that's not required for you to clear it. What matters is that you have located a *Not Mine,* and it needs to go. Imagine the energy leaving in any number of ways:

- Dissolve it into mist and blow it away.
- Vacuum it up and empty the bag into a garbage can.
- Drain it down into the ground, which will then break it down.
- Wrap it up in a package with a "return to sender" sticker on it.
- Comb it out of your field, like removing twigs from your hair.

This awareness can become automatic, as natural as noticing an itch or a muscle ache. In order to function both at home
and out in the world, your first home is inside your own body;
you must be able to keep that space clear and in full alignment with your core.

Anything that that is not yours, that does not belong inside
your edge, will have a disjointed, uneasy, or simply *off* feel to it. It
can feel as though a discordant voice has been added to a harmo-
nious choir. This can also be understood as a frequency or vibration that distorts your own. It might also knock you off balance
or cause you to lose the sense of your *basics*. At some point, when
those skills become more of a habit, you'll be able to stay in balance and recognize problems of ownership much sooner. Here are
some examples:

- A sudden or inexplicable headache
- A flash of a strong emotion that seems unrelated to your
  thoughts
- A surprising physical pain or sensation

The cue might not be dramatic at all—feeling more tired than
expected or simply noticing that a room does not feel welcoming.
These can indicate that you've just encountered something external
that must be negotiated.

Other signs of being at the mercy of something that isn't really
yours can be a sense of burning out; being overloaded in mental, emotional, or energetic ways; feeling off-balance; or not having your usual sense of backbone. It's common to feel crowded,
imposed on, or simply confused. These can also mean that you are
taking on energy from outside, whether you know it or not. You
can learn to manage such places and circumstances.

It's important to recognize that even something you think is benign or safe does not belong inside your personal space; nor is it appropriate for anything of yours to get inside another's edge. This is especially important to remember about people we love. A parent needs to respect the space of a child, and lovers belong next to each other, not enmeshed.

You probably know someone who doesn't recognize boundaries very well. Whether the line crossed is cultural, social, physical, or emotional, there are some clear signals that you are now in uncomfortable territory. In *An Unused Intelligence,* Bryner and Markova list some strong cues that one of your edges has been violated. These cues also point to issues of *ownership.*

- You begin to resist something that didn't bother you before.
- Your hurt feelings linger, even though a situation has been resolved.
- Preoccupied, repetitive reviewing of a conversation or interaction.
- Refusal to change; defensiveness.
- Withdrawing from interactions; starting to withhold information.

In addition to establishing and maintaining your *basics,* there are tools that can help keep you and your energetic anatomy well tuned and responsive. This is the feeling of actually being at home in your self. Chapter 6, "Sanctuary in the Self," will explore some of these skills and how this belonging state comes with a sense of integrity and wholeness.

More about Edges

At the edges of your field or aura are gateways or access points for gathering information. In his book *The Biology of Belief,* author

Bruce Lipton talks about receptor sites, which are located on cell membranes in the human body. They keep the cell healthy by filtering out harmful things and letting good stuff in. Here is what Wikipedia has to say:

> In the field of biochemistry, a receptor is a molecule most often found on the surface of a cell, which receives chemical signals originating externally from the cell. Through binding to a receptor, these signals direct a cell to do something—for example to divide or die, or to allow certain molecules to enter or exit.

It can be helpful to imagine how such receptors might work at the edges of your energetic anatomy. You probably move about in the world knowing that certain things will catch your attention and others won't. This is a reflection of your mental and emotional preferences and interests, and over time your energetic anatomy refines this filtering ability. Your receptor sites become set to screen out certain unwanted information and can draw other sorts of energetic content into your field.

For example, as a "cat person," I will notice and invite cats to approach me, opening up to their personalities and almost automatically engaging in a relationship with them. A dog, on the other hand, unless I have specifically chosen to engage with it, will normally cause my receptor sites to narrow and screen out the less desired (to me!) energy of "dog-ness."

You can learn to determine how you encounter things in the energetic world when you become aware of your own body and how it processes experiences!

My adventures in art museums have already been described, but these kinds of interactions don't have to be that dramatic. Simple, everyday objects also hold information that my awareness, if focused, can pick up. There are different opinions about how much time a person should spend tracking energetic input. Some say your attention is best on alert constantly, but in my experience this is asking too much. I prefer to tune mine to the situation, allowing for a range of intensity that can be quickly adjusted. With experience, I can trust that I'll be alerted to important data by my own sensing anatomy and that if other stuff is screened out, either it is not on my real agenda, or I will learn later and adjust for it.

I have seen very skilled people walking around in states of such high sensitivity that they are in constant reaction to what they encounter out in the world. Each of you will make choices about how, when, and where to use your attention and personal energy. People who do body work, counseling, or other interpersonal services may need a mix of skills quite different from those used by a mechanic or gardener. My hope is that you'll develop the tools in ways that serve to bring you home, wherever you happen to be.

1. Placement Issues

Where you sit in a restaurant or movie theater is a well-known indicator of personal preference. Whether you tend to back up against a wall to watch for gunslingers, sit on the aisle in order to skip out early with minimal disturbance, or enjoy being right in the center, surrounded by your fellow humans, you are doing so based on a reading of the situation's energy and your place within it.

The next time you go out, make a conscious choice to sit somewhere else and notice what your sensing anatomy is telling you. The messages may seem entirely logical and rational, but underneath you will find a more subjective and visceral set of responses. The seat in the center of a long row may feel totally squeezed or just mildly "off." Your system is telling you what it needs to feel right. Now you can go back to the seat that works, knowing that your body is providing you with feedback about something outside you, and you get to manage your reaction and seat choices. With new awareness, those choices may be different!

2. Emotional Ownership

There are times when I discover that a feeling is not even mine to address, much less fix. It belongs to another person, and I have begun to resonate with it. At the post office one busy morning, I was momentarily chagrined to find a line of at least fifteen people snaking around the counter and out the glass double-doors into the entrance lobby. I adjusted my expectation of getting out again quickly and told myself to relax.

The other people in line were in all different states of relaxation themselves. After glancing at them and all the packages and envelopes they carried, I began checking out the brightly colored posters and signage for new stamps. As I stood there, a wave of tension began washing over me. It was as if I were about to leap off a cliff or make some crucial decision, and it did not match my attitude of purposeful patience with the situation.

In that same moment, I noticed my own well-known physical markers for stress; tight jaw, hunched shoulders, restless and irritable thoughts. Even though my hope for a quick stop was clearly thwarted, this reaction was over the top. The clincher was the onset of a headache that I'd not had when parking in the post office lot. Sudden out-of-sync responses like this can be an indicator of an *ownership* problem or issues with your energetic edges. What to do?

First, in *any* situation that feels off, uncomfortable, or out of balance, I check my *basics*. Am I grounded, with a solid sense of my core and cleanly defined edges? Well, I thought I was, but on reflection I saw that in my decision to "relax" into the wait, I had opened up to a lot of information about the people and packages around me. There were a few rather impatient people, fidgeting and anxiously watching for their turn to move forward.

Looking again at my own field, I silently spoke my name into the field around my body and scanned for anything that did not belong. Sure enough, the intense sense of stress and anxiety just didn't seem to fit me. It could have been generated by someone else in the line, but I didn't have to analyze this or concern myself with the source; the main point was that I could recognize that it was not really *mine.*

At times like this, my ability to be aware of what is happening is tested. From here I can step into my own authority by taking responsibility for how I respond to circumstances. Trying to address the source of my unease in a post office is not very practical. Once I know my edges have slipped and I do not even own this degree of stress, I have the freedom to adjust my experience.

Understanding how this can happen in a situation of unexpected close proximity, I made a mental picture of the unease and anxiety being drained out of my system into the earth below my feet, leaving my field clear and filled with only what belongs to me. The budding headache vanished, and the line continued to move. As you begin to practice these skills out the world, it becomes easier to read your surroundings and moderate the impact of outside energies.

Being the Tree

In the "tree exercise" earlier in this chapter, you were introduced to a way of thinking about your body as a physical tool for perceiving and managing energy. As a tree, you can draw support from the ground you have established. But because you are also a human being, you can take those roots with you anywhere and even establish new roots where you go! As a tree, you can use the leaves of your awareness to gather and process information from your surroundings. This establishes your authority over how you respond to the world and the freedom of moderating its effects on you.

Now that you can see the "woods" around you, it's possible to adjust the environment that is yours to manage, your home. You can begin with clutter issues or organization of rooms and belongings and also explore the messages that your body is now picking up about the spaces you live in. Now that you have some tools for coming home to the nested layers of your body, home, and belongings, let's return to the internal nested home of your *self.* This is the *being* part of being at home.

Chapter 6

Sanctuary in the Self
The Nested Layers of Body and Internal Self

You must have a room or a certain hour or so a day where you don't know what is in the newspapers that morning. . . . A place where you can simply experience and bring forth what you are and what you might be. . . . At first you may find that nothing happens there. But if you have a sacred space and use it, something eventually will happen.

—*The Power of Myth,* by Joseph Campbell

Finding your place in the world, creating a home that supports you, and feeling that you belong in the body you have—all these rest on a foundation of alignment. In chapter 5, you encountered the concepts of authority and freedom, which are tools for moving in the world with more ease and confidence. Next we'll introduce and expand on a handful of techniques that will help you stay aligned while you explore the energetic information all around you.

Once you can better manage your own personal energy anatomy, you'll be able adjust the energy in an environment.

The process of finding sanctuary in your *self* begins when you recognize what it means to be aligned with your own integrity. It is the feeling of knowing that your core is connected to your "Ideal Self." Some people take this beyond to their personal conception of source, unity, or God. Now that you have a sense of what your *basics* feel like, you'll start with them and expand into this awareness of your alignment.

People tend to lose their connection to this central self and allow events, other people, and issues in the world affect them. Sometimes this can feel positive, such as when you are praised, congratulated, or simply seen in ways that reinforce what you believe is true about your personality. It is also possible for outside influences to damage or twist this sense of identity.

Take note: your "true, authentic, deepest" self *cannot be harmed or altered in any way.* This essence, call it soul, spirit (whatever suits your worldview), is not the same as your personality or your mental, emotional, or even intellectual identity. What does get affected, for better or worse, is how you navigate everyday life. The personality you use for these daily functions is sort of like the clothes you wear. Knowing the difference between this identity and your essence or higher self is important. There is a relationship between the two, and becoming conscious of it gives you the ability to inhabit your life as well as your home.

How do you realign with that ultimate and essential you, which has taken form in the body that you live in? I want to emphasis that you *live in* a body. Clearly it's your body, but do you really live inside it? *Inhabiting* your body is the key to alignment and finding home where you are.

The location of the human soul or spirit has never been ascertained. Consciousness itself is illusive and subject to much debate.

Wherever it resides, most of humanity can sense that essence that is the basis for religion, philosophy, and personal awareness. You can step into relationship with this part of yourself through meditation, spiritual practices, and in your dreams. Imagine that there is a kind of blueprint, or energetic map, of who you are in the physical body you inhabit. This map or image is a picture of your *being* in its most perfect, balanced, and healthy state. By referencing this image, you can use your awareness and intention to recalibrate your current state to match it and settle back into alignment with your essence.

Lynda Caesara calls this your *Template of Perfection.* This powerful concept points to a central issue for many humans. How do you live with full integrity in all circumstances and situations? Awareness of your Template of Perfection can become one of your *basics,* a steady reminder of who you are and what matters. It is also a useful mechanism for coming back home to your own most vital self. Once again, if you are not comfortable with visualizations, you can consider this exercise a metaphor for the process of realignment.

EXERCISE
Personal Alignment

Settle in a comfortable position and establish your connection to *ground,* your own *core,* and the *edges* surrounding you. Check that within your boundaries there is only *you* and remove anything you do not own using the methods in chapter 5. Once your basics are in place, visualize the energy of the earth nourishing and supporting you, and become settled in your body.

Imagine that your core, which is grounded solidly to the earth, is also reaching up through the top of your head. It extends upward out of the physical into the dimension of your Highest Self. On the way to that most essential expression of who you are, you'll find your Template of Perfection. This template contains the specific information that relates your highest self to the body you inhabit right here, right now. Place your attention firmly on this map and instruct your body to match it in every detail. You are aligning yourself with your own pattern of health, wisdom, balance, purity, and ultimate integrity.

This state is beyond physical limitations and is not defined by the needs of your ego or personality. As you recalibrate yourself to this template, feel yourself return to the state of perfection that reflects your highest self. You may notice that the demands of the mind and emotions quiet down, as the deeper, abiding aspects of your being become clearer. Now you can manage circumstances and situations that accord with that self rather than your accumulated fears and emotions.

This stance is yours, sacred, and personal: an alignment that supports *being home.*

Ideally, everything you do with your physical and energetic bodies is informed by your Template of Perfection. It becomes a reference point for conscious balance and wholeness that you can call on throughout the day. You may find that your connection to it tends to slip when you're under duress or simply preoccupied by events. With time, any feeling of unease or stress will become a reminder to check the condition of your *basics* and *alignment.* If you know that a situation or person may trigger strong feelings, knock you off center, or present some challenge to your sense of integrity or comfort, stop and check your condition first. You can engage them with grace and confidence having taken time to realign your personal energy anatomy.

This invitation to come home to your self has far-reaching implications. It will support you to examine not only your environment, but your own thinking, emotional balance, and the use of your will. By finding sanctuary in the nested layers of your body and internal self, you'll gain clarity about your own attitudes and choices. Issues of time management and information overload can be directly addressed when you learn how to listen to the cues of your body and being. This chapter presents tools for becoming unstuck and learning to call on resources that will empower you at home and in the world outside your door.

Being in Time or on Time

If you can imagine both a time and a place that are dedicated to stillness in your life, finding and living in your aligned core becomes much easier. Your approach to time and the management of it are also worth exploring. Do you spend a lot of your energy trying to "find time" for things? It may seem obvious, but there is really nowhere to locate more time . . . other than right in front of you. The issue goes beyond how to divide it up, because it is essentially *one thing*. Your mind creates the budget and the limits, based on your priorities and the circumstances you face.

In her book *Time*, Eva Hoffman discusses how temporal ordering is needed for language development. In order to describe our experience, we must place it in a sequence, just like the words we use. Living in a sequence of moments allows people to process incoming information. UCLA researchers have found that the brain shifts activity between its different parts in order to process multiple tasks. It engages visual processing and physical coordination to the detriment of areas that are known to handle memory and learning. You might be doing three things at once, but you probably won't remember them all. Multitasking is really a myth.

Problems with time awareness and the ability to be still are hallmarks of attention deficit issues. My definition of this syndrome, whether or not it is diagnosed as ADD or ADHD, is *difficulty sustaining a behavior over time if interrupted by a thought or a visual distraction.*

Our society has managed to just about eliminate delayed grati-
fication. And in those cases where one has to wait, it is considered
a price to pay, a downside. This attitude has radically changed the
way we perceive and use time. In the past, one had to wait for the
TV to warm up, the food to be cooked, the transportation system
(whether a covered wagon or jet) to get us somewhere. We have
shrunk time and flattened it to instant downloads, on-demand TV,
and Internet shopping.

We have closed the gap between here and there, now and later.
John Tomlinson writes in *The Culture of Speed* that there used to be
a separation between what we desire and what we expect to receive,
which was preserved by the necessity of effort. People had to plan
and deploy a series of steps over time in order to get to the goal or
obtain the prize. The way things are now, that gap is minimized.
This may be why more ADD and ADHD occur in people of all
ages. We now have a society in which people can mature without
ever learning to *wait*. One problem is that the volume and speed of
our world is just too much for many to handle.

If a person is encouraged to learn a skill early in life that takes
time and practice—playing a musical instrument or speaking
another language, perhaps—they may be better equipped for our
"culture of speed." But the environment has to support this development of patience and structure. The ability to manage deliberate
learning and attention is part of placing value on something beyond
the demands of the immediate moment. It's a broader viewpoint
that may need to be *cultivated and nurtured*. Here is one way.

Listening and Meditation

There are constant cues and alerts about your environment
all around you. The instrument you use to gather and respond to
them is, as you now know, your body and being. Meditation is one
way to listen with that instrument. As Joseph Campbell asserts, by

establishing a regular and defined pattern of stillness somewhere in your day or week, you create a platform in time and space that supports your awareness of your surroundings and your place in them. Even though it's a common term, meditation inspires reactions that are not always informed. For some it conjures a vision of the swami, heedless of the world, sitting wrapped in his own little sacred universe and somehow more evolved than those mortals who still have to feed the cat and clean the toilet. The stillness that meditation requires is not "better" than action; it is the other half of a whole—just as day and night give each other meaning. Dropping periodically into simple being, our daily *doing* can become much more than an endless grind of chores and rewards.

Another common misconception about meditation is that the goal is to stop your thoughts. Let me assure you right now that this is not the expectation. Yes, advanced meditators do experience a feeling that time has stopped, and, yes, the mind will quiet down, but this is a gradual and lifelong practice. Getting started doesn't have to involve any sort of spirituality or belief system. It is a practical way to harness your busy mind and creative attention. Another part of your experience that may be affected by meditation is the passage of time. You may become more able to manage distraction, irritation, boredom, or restlessness.

In *The Time Paradox,* authors Zimbardo and Boyd describe different ways of thinking about time and how you focus attention on it:

- The past in a negative way: I never have enough money, and it's because of my childhood.
- The past in a positive way: Everything was great back when I was in school.
- The present in a hedonistic, pleasure-seeking way: All that matters is buying this car!

- The present in a fatalistic, "what's the use" attitude: So what if I go into debt, it's too late.

- The future in a planning and strategic way: If I pay off the loan, I can get it next year.

- The future in a "transcendent" approach, geared toward rewards after death: As long as I know that I am using the car for good works, it will all work out somehow.

Most people try to create balance between these types of thinking and do understand when the styles are more or less healthy. But there is a seventh way of relating to time, and here is where it gets interesting: "Holism is the absolute present . . . and is very different from the Western linear view of time. The absolute present contains both past and future. *The present is neither a slave to the past nor a means to the future.* Daily meditation gives the practitioner the experience of being in the present moment, unfiltered through the lens of the past or future."

Zimbardo and Boyd claim that holistic time awareness is both unusual and mostly seen in meditators. The hallmark of this approach is being absolutely present, right here and now. While including awareness of both past and future, the present is not defined by history nor is it just a means to some imagined outcome. Somehow the process of meditation helps people to experience being in the present in a more functional way, not hindered by stories and not defined by longing or unrealistic expectations. It puts you right *here,* where real decisions are made and problems can be solved.

Even though meditation has become a household word that's visible on magazine racks everywhere, it is still not that popular or practiced in our busy Western society. When you are focused on the mind-set of "doing and having," the very idea of slowing down enough to be totally present is somehow risky. You might miss something, lose track of some communication thread, or get left behind.

If you look at those six other kinds of time experience, which one is your default mode? I am sure most of us bounce around among several, but how much of that is a conscious choice? By teaching your body to be still for a defined period of time, you can develop a muscle of awareness that in turn helps you clarify your thinking. This cultivating of *holistic time* places your awareness right here where you are and helps you to stay aligned within your sensory and energetic anatomy.

EXERCISE
Being Still

Set a small timer or alarm for some period of time. Twenty-five minutes is a typical period in many traditions, but if you are new to meditation, start with something you know will be a challenge, but that you are really willing to commit to. Five minutes can be enough to help you realize the power of your own distractibility. Using a timer will take the decision to stop out of your hands, since constant glancing at the clock will erode the process. It is important to rest in the actual experience, rather than monitor it!

Establish your energetic *basics* first. You'll want to be comfortable, since the core skill set is to not move for a determined period of time. It is important to have your back straight and your neck and head comfortable. Sitting in a chair is the simplest way to begin, with your feet flat on the floor and your hands simply resting in your lap. Crossing legs and arms tends to result in some sort of pressure and then you'll need to shift around. There is not a right or wrong way to do this, however; some people like to lie down, and some prefer to meditate while they walk. One thing to watch out for is closing your eyes. In the technique I recommend, you keep your eyes open, but relaxed, gazing softly at the floor in front of you. Meditation is focused, not floating, and having closed eyes can lead to drift or outright sleep.

Next you start by counting your breath. This is the most basic and powerful way to begin, because we *always* have our breath right here. How you count is less important than starting again after ten. Yes, you are counting one to ten, over and over. You can count each inhalation and exhalation, or count each pair as one, but always up to ten, over and over. Here is the reasoning:

This process is not about reaching ten, but about each breath as you take it. This is not as easy as it may seem and works really well as a gauge of when you lose track. For me this becomes clear as I realize I am counting twenty-seven, twenty-eight . . . It's important to remember that you're not trying to "get to ten" so that you can start over. You are holding the number *one* in your mind and body and letting it fill your awareness. As you take the next breath, you become *two* . . . then *three*.

Try to remember a time you had to concentrate completely on a task or a sound, say the sound of a distant motor or a voice in another room. Your whole body leans in and *listens*. That is what this counting is like—*being* the number.

Don't become discouraged and give up when you suddenly realize you are counting in the thirties and thinking about a phone call you have to make later. Simply and gently return again to the number one.

At long meditation retreats, leaders will occasionally remind the whole room of quiet people to return to *this* moment from wherever they may have wandered in their heads. This coming back is a process that continues endlessly. Meditation reveals where our thoughts have run out of control. Here is an analogy for dealing with a busy mind:

Imagine a vast train station—Grand Central Station, perhaps, or any in a big city. If you stand in the huge, empty hall long enough, a train is bound to rumble in on the tracks. It will roar to a stop in front of you and seem very important. Here's the choice: Do you get on and go wherever it takes you or wait, watching until it roars off out the door to disappear in the distance?

The station is your mind, and the trains are thoughts. They will go on their way if you choose not to hop on. Once you get on the train of a thought, you are swept away to next week's interview or yesterday's confrontation in the parking lot. Once you hear the thought and start to feel the emotion of that thought, you have another choice! Return to your breath again and start with one, then two, and so on.

This process is natural, and there is nothing wrong with getting swept away; it will happen. The goal, again, is not stopping all thoughts but gently, over and over, allowing these natural occurrences to rise up and fall away. When you sit still for ten, twenty, or thirty minutes, you may experience physical sensations arising and passing away. This provides concrete and personal proof of how fleeting your thoughts and feelings are.

For example: The sensation of an itch building will take over completely and become my entire experience for several minutes. Gradually, even if I don't scratch, the itch will end. Where did it go? What now? The ticking clock, movement in another room—these sounds fill the universe while I meditate. And they also pass away. By sitting still for these kinds of events, I can come to see that my thoughts come up and pass away, too—if I let them.

This is the power of sitting still. You can watch your mind in all its invention and passion as it presents reasons not to sit still. If you persevere, you'll realize that all thinking, like physical sensations, arises and falls away. This is the bottom line of meditation. Where is your mind now? Is it in the room with the rain on the roof, the person before you, the book at hand?

A last word to skeptics: As weird as it may seem to stop doing things in order to perform better, meditation is a practical tool that can help you harness energy and focus on what really matters to you. It can help you recognize when you are distracted and make better choices about what to do next. I invite you to experiment with a few minutes a day.

Five minutes to start is good, and build up to fifteen or twenty. In fact, I sometimes just take *two minutes* to remind myself that I can actually adjust my attitude if I choose. You can stop, take a single breath, and then begin with more clarity and presence. Perhaps just those two minutes of stillness in the middle of your personal whirlwind will make all the difference.

Processing Incoming Information

How do you deal with the endless stream of incoming information of daily life? On one hand, all this data seems to hit us from the outside, coming from people, the media, and the places you live and work. It can feel like you are being bombarded and have no place to turn. For some, this results in wanting to close off the flow, but I would like to propose that moderating this constant influx can be best done from the inside out.

Rather than separating from it, you can use your energy anatomy to moderate what you allow in. Rather than being too sensitive to all the environmental factors, you can choose how to respond when you are aware of what is possible. As you now know, mind, body, and feeling are linked, and it's crucial to remember that you have more than your intellect at hand.

In *Self Comes to Mind,* which was referenced in chapter 2, Antonio Damasio examines consciousness—how we use it and define ourselves by it. He describes an experiment by Ap Dijksterhuis that compares the use of conscious and unconscious mental processing in the task of choosing between two objects. The subjects had to make a range of decisions, from picking out a toaster to the more involved selection of a family car. Some subjects were encouraged to use care and methodical deliberation, while others were distracted from the process in an attempt to measure how a less-focused state of mind would affect their choices. What role might intuition or the unconscious play in different scenarios?

While rational thought and intuition ideally support each other, the test indicated some surprising variations on how it might work. As far as the big ticket choices were concerned, better decisions were made in the "distracted" state. Damasio believes that the unconscious mind appeared to have more "space" for operating. Perhaps this state is less subject to the complications of emotional or historical filters. He calls this "nonconscious" processing and reminds readers that we actually use it to perform many skills that are learned in the "clear light of consciousness, but which then go underground into the roomy basement of the mind," like driving a car or making coffee before actually waking up.

In another experiment about the role of nonconscious mind, Damasio found a way to measure a decision that happens *before* the conscious mind really knows what it is doing. Card players with a pair of stacked decks showed measurable skin conductance changes just prior to selecting a card from the losing pile. Without being able to say why, these people would switch and select a card from the other option, a winning deck. Damasio proposes that at some nonconscious level, the players got a jolt from the basement of their minds, one which not only affected measurable skin conditions but which amounted to an intuition that one deck was a bad choice. He uses the word *intuition* for the delivery of a solution that did not involve conscious mental processing or deliberation.

Most people "know in their bones or guts," which are certainly parts of their bodies, that intuition is a real sensation. But how much can you trust it, even though some responses are possible to measure? The intellect can dress up the feeling of a churning tummy with a rational backstory, but this denies the power of your body as a sensing tool. Understanding this may help you give your own flashes of nonconscious information more credence. At the very least, your intuition can become another source for moving in the world with awareness.

Attitude and Choice

Ways of thinking physically include recognizing that I must change myself before I can affect someone else. This requires increased awareness of what I do habitually and what my real intentions are in any given interaction.

—*An Unused Intelligence,*
by Andy Bryner and Dawna Markov

It's tempting to think that the weather outside is your baseline for the day ahead. Even more typical is letting the mood of your morning color the hours until bedtime. While weather and mood certainly have a role to play, neither should get the job of defining your experience without some consideration.

The tone of your day is determined by you, starting with an accurate self-assessment and knowing your real priorities. Without this crucial information, there will be no way to change circumstances or interact with other people in a clear, intimate, or effective way. Learning to determine your own attitudes is a doorway to freedom, right here. The challenge is to recognize what you start out with, what is so close that you don't even see it as a filter or barrier between yourself and circumstances. Driving in traffic is a great place to look for conditioned attitudes.

For years I operated on what felt like the unassailable assumption that if someone was in my way, they were doing it on purpose. If I really looked at this, my intellect could dismiss it, but the emotional charge was much harder to let go. This was a lens through which I saw anything that thwarted my plans; any delay or frustration was an event directed at me, specifically.

This pattern of thinking had consequences for my physical state; tension being just a starting point. My clenched jaw and tight shoulders directly reflected a mental and emotional state that I wanted to change and became a built-in reminder to look deeper. Wanting to react with less physical stress led to an examination of the hidden attitudes I drove around with in traffic. Owning my attitude made it possible to change my whole approach to circumstances, especially the ones I have no real way to control.

What does it mean to own my attitude? When I am truly at home in my body and self, I can recognize that the feelings of frustration come from inside *in reaction* to what I experience in the world. It takes practice, but as my internal weather changes, I can tell the difference between it and the conditions that trigger it. Right there is the opening; I choose to return to a calm state, maybe even laugh at myself, and accept that I am in fact stuck in traffic, period. Instead of open freeway lanes (or lack of them) determining the direction of my morning, I am able to bring my day into line with both intention and a bit more grace.

And when I do lose that perspective and react in old ways to frustrations, I can ask: How did I let circumstances define my context again? My history, the lenses I look through, or the triggers for my frustration are right there to see, if I am willing to look inside instead of outside. It's not about dwelling in endless self-justification, either. Instead I can move through circumstances into the possibility of change. From here, I can restore balance and my personal alignment.

Attention, Intention, No Tension

This useful phrase can help stop a spiral of thinking or feeling that is not healthy or that is keeping you in a frustrating or stuck place. You walk yourself through the three steps like this:

- **Attention:** What you put your attention on grows stronger and is fed by your awareness, whether it's positive or negative. So recognize what you are really *feeding!*

- **Intention:** Focus on a clear picture of what you choose to create. It may be an actual concrete result, or it can be the shift in attitude that you desire.

- **No Tension:** Let go of your attachment to things outside your real control. You can manage the actions you take, but the final outcome and how it arrives may be totally beyond you.

The point is to clarify your intention without fixating on negativity or too much detail. Once you are clear, your next step may begin to show itself, possibly in unexpected ways. On a practical level, this means doing everything you can think to do, then come back to the third principle . . . let go.

In my driving example it would look like this:

- **Attention:** I am feeding my impatience and irritation by focusing hard on every move the car in front of me makes and filtering it through a demand that I be treated fairly and get my way.

- **Intention:** I turn my attention to the goal of getting to my destination in a calm and relaxed state. Instead of vindication, I choose detachment and avoiding an accident.

- **No Tension:** And besides, all I am really able to manage is my *own* driving; accidents happen, and the best outcome will be to know I did not cause one.

Attitude and choice rely on your ability to recognize self-generated drama and stories. Whether they originated in childhood or have become a way to deal with stress, stuck patterns of belief and thought can limit your options. In fact, these places of resistance can outright blind you to what is really happening.

Zimbardo and Boyd, in *The Time Paradox,* bring up the idea that people define their own memories based on what they believe to have happened. How accurate is your information? If you examine your past, you may find that some memories reflect events in ways that suit you without being totally accurate.

An example: I recently realized that while I believe I was happy and excited to return from a month-long visit with relatives when I was sixteen, I have no actual memory of that six-day trip. None. What was I doing? It was a complicated and dramatic journey down the coast of Norway on ships, trains, and boats. That period of time is a blank page in my mind, so why do I still cling to idea that I was so pleased at the time? It may not matter at all, but it's interesting to note that I have constructed a vivid story for myself—based on zero actual memory!

This can work moving forward in time as well. What you see may rely heavily on what you expect to see or think you know about what is front of you. In *The Art of Possibility,* authors Rosamund and Benjamin Zander reference a comment that Albert Einstein is reported to have made to his colleague Werner Heisenberg. They were talking about the idea that theories are only founded on facts that are observable. Einstein said, "In reality the very opposite happens, it is theory which decides what we can observe."

Consider this: how you think controls what you perceive and how you manage it. Attitude and choice make all the difference.

Getting Stuck on Stories

In order to find your way home to a sanctuary of both inner self and outer environment, you need to know where you stand. One step in that direction is to own your stories and habits.

The feeling of being stuck usually happens in the present. Right now, you just can't move. But there are other places you might get frozen: in your past, in a habit or a trauma. You may also feel stuck in situations with other people or your work. Anneli Rufus tackles the landscape of stuckness head-on in her book, *Stuck: Why We Can't (or Won't) Move On.*

She takes apart the social influences and asks some hard questions. One of the most striking sections looks at ways society has made this trapped state into an accepted condition, a sort of pseudo-fact-of-life.

In lands of plenty, in the lap of luxury, in the fast lane, we're stuck doing—over and over—things we do not want to do. Stuck in places we do not want to be. Stuck with people we do not want to see. Stuck with stuff. Stuck without enough. What irony. You and I will almost surely never be sold into slavery. Those days are gone. We will not become indentured servants, will not be shanghaied and dragged off to sea, locked in the hold, hands chained to oars. We were not betrothed at age ten. That's stuck. In all of history, no population anywhere has ever been so free as we. And yet—somehow we all feel stuck.

In the chapter on habits, she takes herself to task for wearing ragged clothing. She explains that, for her, this reflected a story about not caring what people think. She eventually realized that the disguise of unkempt clothing was a great way to avoid owning her adulthood. Simply put: a great way to not be a grown-up. My own mother would find my fascination with this very amusing. She never understood why I resisted dressing like a girl in those faraway years when daughters dressed like their mothers. I used clothing to resist what I saw as the restricted role of women. Now that I am the captain of my destiny, I actually enjoy dressing up. My story has changed!

Here is the crux of all stuckness, according to Rufus, whether it is in habits, beliefs, relationships, or stuff: "The problem with change is that it requires self-awareness, courage, and effort." As long as the issue is outside you, it is easy to explain its power over you. *When you recognize your own role in a situation, you are coming home to yourself.*

In his book, *The Unfolding Now: Realizing Your True Nature through the Practice of Presence,* A. H. Almaas talks about how staying stuck in a situation implies resistance to who you are. He says that when you reject or hope to get rid of a problem or experience, you are actually preserving it in a form that will be very difficult to get past. Pushing something away, a habit or a story, crystalizes it and blocks you from exploring it or understanding what lies beneath the surface. By focusing on the stuckness or negativity or even your own defensiveness, *you reject reality.* In order to create change or movement, you must start from where you are now, and this requires awareness and acceptance of what is.

How do you recognize stuck places and step into awareness with courage and willingness? It happens when you return to your energetic *basics* and knowledge of your *core.* Alignment is the place to start.

For me, that meant seeing that I told myself a limiting story about how women needed to dress in order to maintain their autonomy and power. This story blocked my way back to the sanctuary of the self at my core. Once I stood firm in my core, it was much easier to recognize that what I wear is a creative choice and can reflect exactly what I want. At bottom, this involved realizing that interpretations others may put on my outfits are not mine to control, either! What freedom!

The self that is your true home is the only one that you never have to leave. This place of belonging is the starting point, yet for many is the hardest place to settle. Identifying your stories and stuck places can be hard, but the reward is living in a place of trust and confidence in where you stand. From this perspective, you can step forward and create home in the places you live and work.

Once at home in who you are, your choices open up. You can say: I am an artist/businessperson/family member. Therefore I choose to keep this, live here, and go to these places. And then life happens.

Self-Righting Techniques

All the best intentions and awareness in the world won't stop the "burning house of daily life" from offering challenges and surprises. Rushing about with fire extinguishers can unsettle the most grounded person. So it's important to have skills and techniques for bringing yourself back to your *core* and into balance, to remember that you are indeed at home anywhere and in all circumstances. With another nod to the personal-energy classes of Lynda Caesara, these are called *self-righting techniques.*

The very first thing to acknowledge is that anytime you feel "off," your *basics* may be compromised. Assess the condition of your *ground, core, and edges* before trying to sort the problem from the outside. By remembering that your most basic place of home is within your body and self, you're better equipped to cope with disturbing places, people, or circumstances. In fact, any sensations of unease, irritation, or imbalance can become your cue to check in. They are nature's little alarm clocks that can *wake you up* to what is happening inside and around you.

Your *basics* are the most fundamental tools for self-righting, but there are many others. They often come packaged with spiritual disciplines and can look like praying, meditations, ceremony, or movement. Some people find one or more paths that suit them. Others tend to gather techniques that work in different ways at different times. One worth describing here is an approach found in many cultures and used throughout measurable time: calling for support from beyond humanity.

Identifying Your Resources and Helpers

By any name—angels, ancestors, minor deities, or fetish spirits—the use of a support team seems wired into human DNA. Some people prefer to go straight to the top and call directly on God, an ultimate higher power, or Divine White Light. Even atheists seem to call on Reason with a capital "R." Whether the assistance comes from within or from out there somewhere in the ether, there is still a reach for the help itself. This reach is the point, and the outfit it wears is secondary.

I personally come from a practice that takes a very strong stand on not having any central focus at all. And yet, within this strain of very traditional Japanese Zen Buddhism, we routinely profess to take refuge in Buddha, Dharma, and Sangha. These are also known as the Three Treasures: the teacher, the teachings, and our fellow practitioners.

The reach is a way of gathering support and making a connection with resources beyond my own. Even if I look within to my own unconscious or innate powers, there is a gesture. The gesture can be a plea for specific result, or it can be a call for understanding. I need help and can I get it now, please?

This resource can be a fun one to cultivate. It can express cultural interests, your family traditions, or anything in between. Becoming aligned with allies can start with something as simple as saying good morning to a tree you enjoy on your commute. It is a process of noticing your own place in the environment and how you interact with what surrounds you.

Another name for allies in one tradition is "stand-behinds," as their job description includes watching your back. One of my teachers was playing with her son and his rubber dinosaur collection. At

one point in the fracas of territory defense, the boy noticed that his
team needed help. He remarked, "I need to get more dinos behind
me." In this example, plastic dinosaurs were holding ground for a
young boy's game strategy, but it reflects a deeper need that most of
us share. You can pick whatever kind of dinos you like.

Probably the most prevalent and understood "stand-behinds"
(besides those of organized religion) are ancestors. The idea is that
by honoring your ancestors, they can protect or guide you in ways
that the living can't. Not all ancestors are appropriate for this job; so
be aware of asking for the blessing or wisdom of the particular family member. Keep in mind that anyone can be a designated ancestor;
blood relations are just one way to determine a connection. They
can be some respected scientist, a beloved poet, or any once-living
person whom you wish to invoke as support. Think of the millions
who reference Mother Teresa when they need to feel compassion.

Another classic from the wisdom of AA (Alcoholics Anonymous) is the practice of starting the morning with a simple, heart-
felt request for help with whatever the day may hold. You can call
it a prayer, an intention, or a plea. Some people recommend asking
while kneeling next to their beds, but I also find that while brush-
ing my teeth is a perfect time to mentally recite daily invocations.
Remembering to simply connect with a source of aid outside your
own thinking is the key. The second half of the AA technique is
ending your day with "Thank you."

One last idea is to request the backing of any group or heritage
that you are either part of or simply admire and respect. I know
people who call upon their martial arts lineage and others who stick
to Mother Nature herself.

At Home in the Sanctuary of Self

All these skills refine your ability to experience the foundational,
essential place of home, the one that can never be taken from you.

Explore your relationship to time as it flows around you. Learn to experience stillness and the power of listening, which will help you process all the world throws at you. This is when your attitude, choice, and stories become conscious tools.

Practice how to self-right in times of stress and overload, and cultivate resources and support beyond your own human limits.

From here you are ready to turn outward again and examine the nested layer of home in the wider world of nature and society.

Chapter 7

The Ambient Home
Clearing Space

We had always done this in the part when the train took that corner into the valley and we yearned to see again the green curve arc of the paddocks . . . with the familiar bulk of the barn behind it.

"It's still the same," Helen said. "How can it be so much the same when we are away from it? Doesn't our presence mean anything?"

—*A House of Trees,* by Joan Colebrook

The fundamental qualities of an environment—*function, layout,* and *energy*—come together and should balance one another in the experience of a typical home. *How* do you achieve this balance?

Balancing the Fundamental Qualities

You've just come in the door and set the mail on the kitchen counter. The cat wants to be fed, and the phone rings. In a skillfully set up environment, there will be a designated place for that mail, with all the tools you need to process it nearby. The cat food will be easy to pull out and pour one-handed, if that is how you manage it more often than not. These aspects of order and layout will support the feeling of being in control, calm, organized, and able to function as the phone keeps ringing.

Now look at the more subjective and energetic quality of this particular domestic moment: your experience of the ringing phone. Does the sound strike you as a choice or a demand? Here is where your sense of being home in your body and self makes a difference. The sound of the phone may be a welcome signal that your children are probably checking in, or it might be a tedious intrusion from a salesperson. Your next move will reflect the extent to which you are at home with your priorities and values. Whether you answer the ringing phone or not, you are making a choice that directly affects your space. In this domestic episode, you can witness the interplay of order, function, and energy. They dance together all the time!

When one or another of the fundamental qualities is not in balance, the result can be frustration and sometimes even a sense of being overwhelmed. Once the aspects of order and function have been addressed, you may still feel lingering energetic unease. Before learning how to clear that energy in your space, let's look at a system that also begins with perception and defines some qualities of spatial energy.

Exploring Deep Modes of Being Home: Tibetan Mudra Space Awareness

There are many books about feng shui and how we Westerners have translated it for use in split levels, condos, and across cul-de-sacs. These approaches tend to define an ideal and explain how to either achieve it or fix a situation to match. I'd like to emphasize that the heart of any system isn't cures and adjustments, it is awareness.

Helen Berliner's book *Enlightened by Design* offers a method based on concepts from Tibetan feng shui. The organization of a space is based on patterns of energy as defined below and how each functions in that space. The moderation and control of these patterns requires attention to existing conditions that can be adjusted in your home. Each of the energies needs to circulate throughout the house, balancing and supporting specific actions in different rooms. The overall balance is the key to their functioning as an *ambient*, or enfolding and surrounding, environment. The following are examples of how these energies are reflected in a home and the world outside.

Space: A relaxed and flexible functioning. When your rooms work, you connect more easily to the sacred in the everyday. Spaces that are too tight or chaotic can constrict this receptivity.

- In the home: open space flowing through the house allows change and the ability to rest, be centered, and sleep well.
- In the world: plazas, malls, open public space—can you navigate easily, see your way?

Clarity: Calms and clarifies energy, giving it form and focus, reducing chaos and frustration. Using boundaries and simplicity, you can establish meaning and priorities.

- In the home: rooms are easy to use, with qualities of peaceful focus.
- In the world: schools, libraries, or hospitals ideally offer a sense of organization and clarity of purpose.

Richness: Well-being and abundance are the focus of richness, affecting your confidence and influence. It can be seen in the diversity, generosity, and splendor of your space.

- In the home: kitchens and dining rooms reflect stability and abundance.
- In the world: décor in restaurants, banks, markets.

Warmth: Friendship and relationships are core elements of life that the space supports by attention to conversation, connection, entertainment, and pleasure.

- In the home: living rooms and entryways welcome, embrace, and reflect the center, heart, or, more traditionally, a sense of the hearth of a home.
- In the world: theaters, restaurants, community spaces entertain and inform with beauty.

Energy: Efficiency, functionality, movement, security are reflected and enhanced by attention to the quality of energy and how it moves in the environment.

- In the home: work surfaces, desks, places for efficiency with flow and vitality.
- In the world: offices, factories, airports; places of production.

Up: The presence of guidance in life, whether it is represented by ancestors, spirituality, or a relationship to a higher power.

Down: The mundane, practical activities of life: cooking, eating, sleeping, banking.

Berliner uses the term *ambient home* to reflect the surrounding, encircling quality of a space designed to create an envelope of belonging. Within that space, you can also apply the same patterns to your physical health. Once again, you return to the instrument you have at hand, your body and its grounded presence.

An ambient home reflects a conscious relationship to your surroundings. This awareness provides the key to creating spaces that truly support you. Here is where things get interesting. You can change how a space feels by giving awareness to what you experience, but only if you are at home already in your body and self. Starting here, you can identify an uncomfortable energy in your environment and recognize that this pattern is not coming from you; it is *outside your edge*.

This is why the concepts and exercises from chapter 3 are so important. Being grounded, standing in your core, and having clear edges will enable you to adjust the energy in the environment. You can think of it as composing your own domain.

Space Clearing Defined

An ambient home is informed by your presence. It is a two-way street. The communication happens at each of the levels discussed in chapter 4: function, layout, and energy.

Clearing is the process of consciously negotiating with your surroundings in order to adjust the *feeling and sense of belonging at home.*

This involves addressing energetic information, which can be thought of as a frequency or a kind of vibration. For example, when a tuning fork is struck and brought close to something vibrating at a lower frequency, the tuning fork causes that object's frequency to shift toward itself, to match the frequency of the tuning fork. The tuning fork entrains the object's vibration and brings it into alignment. This can be demonstrated by touching a vibrating tuning fork to a pane of glass in a window. When lifted away, you will hear the window vibrating at the same frequency as the tuning fork.

In just this way, the clearing process sets up a vibration in the room and shifts the existing frequency to match that chosen for the room. Suddenly things may feel lighter, more open, and realigned. Old patterns of discomfort, anxiety, or restlessness can vanish, clearing the way for other changes and a more vivid sense of *being home*.

Part of clearing is recognizing the difference between your own energy and what comes from outside—the *ownership* skill set. This awareness includes physical cues from your body, as well as mental and emotional input from other people. This can get complex, as it can work both ways. On one hand, you might assume that what you're experiencing is being generated by forces entirely beyond your control. This may lead you to abandon your own skill set and feel like a victim of these situations. On the other hand, some people err on the side of owning everything they encounter, which means they do not recognize how to protect themselves.

While our perceptions do come through our own filters, often what we think is personal comes from the emotional field of another person or the quality of energy associated with a particular place. For example, how might we react to accidentally overhearing an argument? If we are susceptible to the frequency of anger, we may find ourselves automatically going into a defensive posture or beginning to feel a similar, if lesser, state of anger. Not everyone will respond this way, but it helps to identify when and what kind of energetic patterns trigger our own systems.

So how can you learn to recognize the difference between your own inherent energies and those that you encounter? Again, a first step is to stop activity long enough to register your own body. By focusing on your ground, your stance on the earth, you can create a moment in which awareness can flower. The next challenge is to maintain a sense of your actual boundaries, both those defined by your skin and those you establish energetically. These boundaries change and accommodate the situations we are in.

Try watching your comfort level in interaction with people and become aware of how your boundaries accommodate what is happening. Your edge will tend to be closer to your skin when you are feeling safe with someone and farther out if you are threatened. As you might imagine, there are healthy and unhealthy ways that we subconsciously use these energetic boundaries. Any party setting or bus ride will provide demonstrations of people adjusting and reacting to the energetic edges of the people around them.

In learning how to adjust your environment, the initial challenge is just to see how much the external has become "our own" condition. We unknowingly hold existing patterns in place with our attitudes and reactions to them. When we resonate with their frequency, our experience becomes like an amplified sound wave. This is why knowing and maintaining your personal edge and boundary are so important. Your edge helps you know what is yours and what is not.

The Process of Clearing

Start by slowing down enough to register and examine your first impressions of a room or building. Even a place we know well and spend a lot of time in will open up in new ways if we stop our habitual interactions with it. Consider your own bedroom or kitchen. By simply standing still in your kitchen for five minutes, your relationship to it will change. In that time, it is possible to recognize the variety of emotional states you usually experience in the room. The trick is to let the room communicate with you rather than imposing your current mental state on it.

It may also help to address issues of clutter and disorganization ahead of time. Sometimes you can't "hear" the energetic messages without facing the clutter; other times you'll need to clear the energetics before you'll manage the cleanup. This is about your relationship to the space, so you may want to experiment with different approaches.

The Steps

- Have your basics in place: ground, core, and edges.

- Check personal alignment and your ability to process information. Are you comfortable? Not distracted? Able to focus on where you are right now?

- Be clear on whom the clearing is for, because the goal is to align the room with the person living in or using it.

- Listen first. What is the space saying about order and layout?

- Pay attention to the energetic content without losing your perspective or ability to stand aside and receive information about it.

- Visualize disruptive qualities being removed, released, or drained away from the space. Use imagery that suits the occupants.

- Imagine a frequency that supports and honors the occupants. Visualize it being large enough to entrain the whole room, and establish a new and healthy alignment with the occupants.

Your intuition and sensitivity will open a channel to the space itself. It may provide you with verbal information or an image in your mind's eye. This example will illustrate the process.

The Cottage Clearing

A client and her partner brought me in to help with fine-tuning the energetics of their jewel box of a cottage home. The project involved some extensive remodeling and the combining of their two households. We had already done some preliminary energetic clearing, looking at the land itself and any remaining influences from the previous owners. At this point, things were feeling quite balanced, even though I had the sense from the building that the changes felt like having a Band-Aid pulled off, a bit stressful but ultimately for the best.

One room in particular caught my attention. This space was planned as a place to relax and would eventually include a ship's ladder to a loft area. We knew that the *function* aspect had been addressed; the purpose of the room was clear and the furniture would support that. The *layout* was not ideal with the traffic pattern to the bedroom running through the middle, but this was not really a major issue. So what had snagged my awareness? As I stood there feeling the quality of the room, I recognized that there might be an *energetic* issue. The room felt uneasy and somehow off-balance.

In order to listen objectively to the pattern of unease I felt, I first put my *basics* in place and then felt my connection to my clients, mentally bringing forward my understanding of their individual history and shared story. The clearing was about their relationship to the cottage, and it was important to clearly define my role as a facilitator for them. Any attempt to adjust energy must support the priorities and feelings of the people involved. But it's actually less about "knowing" this information than it is *holding the intention* to reflect it as an energetic frequency. This is like selecting the right tuning fork for the job.

Next I imagined that information pouring into the room and visualized the room as a container to hold the homeowners and their desire to live in the house. In my mind's eye, this would help the building become a unique, deep, and meaningful expression of who they are. Once that felt solid, I asked the room itself to match that information. Depending on how you relate to energetic data, this can be thought of as a frequency adjustment or a shift in tone. The process was one of respectful invitation—asking that the rooms join the occupants in creating an ambient home.

As we stood there together, I felt the room seem to acknowledge us. Any space can become a finely tuned refuge, nurture its inhabitants, and support their well-being. This is what I felt happening. People will process this kind of change with the unique energy anatomy of their own. For me the air molecules became brighter, the sense of visible light increased, and colors sharpened. I experienced a tangible expansion of spatial volume, as if the room became bigger and denser at the same time.

The beauty of the process was the moment when the owners also recognized that space and began to feel it reflect their presence. They had become responsible for what they brought to the room on the levels of function, layout, and energy. The same loft that a moment before had felt cut off and unavailable became linked to the room below by the now clearly formed intentions of the occupants. Since the space was now aligned with them, the loft joined with the energy of the whole room, even before the ladder was installed. The clerestory window above lit up the whole space, reflecting the dreams of the inhabitants for the future.

This is the moment in an energetic clearing when the inhabitants feel their core encounter the realigned energy of the environment. It's a true homecoming with awareness.

By inhabiting your body and whole self, you have the ability to navigate your home and any surroundings with energetic confidence. Shall we step out into the wider world?

Chapter 8

Belonging Everywhere
The Nested Layers
of Nature and Society

The mind is trying to find its place within the land, to
discover a way to dispel its own sense of estrangement.
—*Arctic Dreams,* by Barry Lopez

Moving Out into the World with Tools of Awareness

Once you inhabit the nested layers of body, self, and home with
a degree of confidence and awareness, you can step out into nature
and society with greater ease and comfort. Places that aren't yours
to control will become a measure of your skills. This chapter will
cover some techniques that make it possible to create sanctuary for
yourself wherever you happen to be. The use of energetic skills can
become a very practical and almost automatic tool for recognizing
and relating to *all* the places you go.

By exploring and developing your awareness of the energy centers or chakras, for example, you'll find that they can function as

organs of perception. In the following example, you'll see how they worked for me at the museum.

Example: Back to the Museum

An example of using your basics, as well as understanding and managing an experience in the wider world, can be seen in a story you already know—my adventure in the art museum. To recap: I had begun to feel unsettled and restless after about fifteen minutes of *taking in* (important wording) the bright and eccentric images in Frida Kahlo's paintings.

The discomfort came out of nowhere very fast, and my first and most natural impulse was to wonder what I had eaten or if I was coming down with something. The discomfort was not like a stomachache, however; it felt more like I had suddenly slipped a disk or fallen down the stairs. It felt like an injury. I sat down and realized that I was experiencing a problem of *ownership*. How did I know? Finding my *basics* was the first priority: ground, core, and edges. Once I looked for the condition of my edges, it was obvious that I had let them widen and almost disappear in order to become open to the art I was enjoying.

This is a natural response to beauty, but it also exposed me to a whole range of information that I was not expecting. At this point, I didn't know that the artist had lived through a terrible back injury and was creating paintings for many years while experiencing excruciating pain. I had picked up not only the messages within the images, but the agony behind the creation of those works. I had to reestablish my edges and close off the flow of energetic data to my system.

After grounding and locating my core, things began to improve, and I could straighten up. The next step was to pull my edges in, and I imagined that the membrane surrounding me had become more dense, a thicker skin between me and everything else. Next

I held the intention to get rid of whatever was not really mine, to let it drain out quickly through the bottoms of my feet. I felt much better within several minutes and could move around without wincing.

But how was I going to manage the rest of the museum visit? Certainly I could go back and look at the exhibit, keeping my edges in place, but I also wanted to enjoy the paintings fully. I don't want to be controlled by energies that I can learn to manage. In my experience, many people encounter something like this and decide that it's too much, choosing to step back from anything uncomfortable or negative in any way. There is another way!

Once the information about Kahlo's pain was out of my energetic anatomy, it did not feel dangerous or at all threatening. Instead it was just another piece of information in the space of the museum, along with the other people and their fields.

Then I remembered that I could also adjust how much I let into my system by imagining that I had a filter over my second energy center or chakra. This is the point at which emotionally charged information can enter and overwhelm my system. I imagined a filter covering it that could be adjusted in the way a camera lens is opened or closed to let in light. This worked well with some practice, and in this way I could walk through the museum knowing that a lot was happening in the paintings and yet also feel confident that I was not being energetically overwhelmed. This was just one way to handle that situation, as you will see.

More on Using Fibers and Intention

In the museum example, I mention forming a thought and holding an intention several times. This is the moment when you step into your own authority and relationship with your surroundings. Being at home in your body and familiar with your own particular and unique energetic anatomy brings you to this place of sanctuary in your aligned self. Now you can choose to connect with the environment by using your will and attention. This involves a more conscious understanding of how fibers work.

Chapter 3 described fibers as one leg of a three-legged stool of perception. The first leg is your physical body for sensing and gathering information. The second is your internal experience of mind and emotion. The third leg of the stool is the human energetic system and a component called fibers, which are tools of your will and reflect your intentions. At first you may not always be aware of what you're doing with them! The museum encounter is a great example for this as well.

I had attached myself to the paintings with fibers that connected my energy anatomy directly to the paintings and all they contained. This is just what people do when they are interested or curious. After realizing the amount of pain with which Kahlo had imbued her work, I learned a lesson about my own capacity in museums.

Consider the fact that when you direct your attention toward any object, the action starts in your mind with an impulse or thought. At some point, you may form the intention to move toward the object; this can be either conscious or below the threshold of your internal mental dialog. The attention you have paid to the object and any intention to act may result in movement across the room. Attention and intention can lead to real, measurable results or remain as energetic impulses or ideas. Where do fibers enter the picture? They are the connection between the intention in your mind (the energetic) and the physical world, whether the results affect just your body or involve other objects.

Whether you create a physical change or not, the fibers exist as extensions of your energy anatomy. You can learn to place them on objects that you choose to interact with, and you can pull them back into your own field, which can break the connection. The more rational-minded might question that our energetic fibers also move out away from our bodies in ways that affect people and things. This is one of those places where experience and interpretation of your own sensations will be your guide.

Fibers and People

Consider arriving at a party. You only know the host and a couple other people. At the door, you are casting your fibers out in a scan of the room, either with awareness or not. Remember that by directing your attentions, you have attached a fiber of attention from yourself to an object or person. Sometimes it's just how you function in the day-to-day world, but if you look deeper, you'll see other applications of your fibers. At the party, your fibers may return information about who might be safe to approach. In fact, as you scan the room, those same fibers may draw the attention of someone who suddenly turns to see you. Conscious use of your fibers in personal interactions is a useful skill, one explored in detail in *Hands of Light,* by Barbara Ann Brennan.

The unconscious ways you engage friends and associates can be especially revealing. You can probably tell whether someone is really listening or is actually trying to end a conversation. People read these signs all the time and call it intuition or sensitivity or simple social skills.

Physical objects may not roll across the table toward you when you focus your fibers on them, but your intention to locate your keys may intensify your link to them and seem to draw you toward them. By developing skill with your fibers, you may not be able to control the universe, but you will probably feel more connected to your immediate surroundings.

Nature

How do birds find home? According to researchers Le-Qing Wu and David Dickman at the Baylor College of Medicine (article in the *New York Times,* April 2012, by James Gorman), there are cells in the brains of pigeons that record detailed information about the earth's magnetic field, rather like a "biological compass." Birds sense the data and compare it to a stored map in their brains. The Baylor researchers have identified a group of cells in the birds that record the direction and strength of the magnetic field, and they believe it's in the inner ear of the birds. It remains to be confirmed, but the most likely candidate for the location of the internal map is the hippocampus, the part of the brain involved in memory in both birds and humans.

This recalls a study showing that experienced London taxi drivers who have memorized the complex street layout of that city have a larger hippocampus than new drivers who have not mastered the system. While the magnetism study does not answer the question of how the information is monitored by the inner ear, it clearly supports the theory that it's getting into the brain somehow and being used to navigate across long distances.

In *Healing Spaces: The Science of Place and Well-Being,* Esther M. Sternberg looks in depth at how human brains respond to environmental features and which features tend to promote healing. Color, sounds, temperature, texture, depth of field, and light all play roles. Sternberg describes one link to nature itself that is found in the measurable response people tend to have to fractal patterns in the world outside.

> Such branching, self-similar patterns that occur repeatedly in increasingly smaller scales are found throughout nature, not only in trees but also in waves, snowflakes, seashells, and flowers. They are called fractals. . . . Other fractal structures in nature include mountains ranges, coastlines, the veins in leaves, and the cells in the human body.

Fractals appear in art and architecture and would seem to be intrinsically soothing to the human mind. In 1996, a paper by Ary Goldberger, a professor of cardiology at Harvard Medical School, proposed this idea and referenced such examples as Gothic cathedrals and the art of Katsushika Hokusai. In Hokusai's well-known painting of Mount Fiji, the curlicue pattern of waves repeats almost endlessly in smaller and smaller scales.

Goldberger thinks that such patterns, with their complex and repetitive movement of scale, serve to free up the mind, allowing it to both relax and move inward or outward, up or down. Goldberger also did studies of how heart rate is affected by visual and auditory information. Although few conclusive tests exist, it appears that these environmental factors can influence healing and well-being.

As you become more aware of how objects, rooms, and buildings affect your sense of comfort, another source of home and belonging may be found outside your door in nature itself. Two examples of the soothing power of fractals are trees and water. By finding your own favorite expression of nature, you can find your way back to that largest and most encompassing nest of home, the earth itself.

I have two such "portals," as I think of them, both easy to get to from my back door. The first is a madrona tree in my garden, and the other requires a short walk up over a hill to a view of Puget Sound. By touching the tree with my hand or the moving water with my eyes, I move back into alignment with nature and a home much bigger than anywhere I might actually hang my hat. Here is where the fractal and interconnected aspect of nature plays a role: any tree or any water I encounter is linked to my sense of home. *And thus, any tree or any water, anywhere, will help me feel at home.*

A living tree or untamed water work best for me, but a closed room, a stuffy jet plane, or a city street are part of the web as well.

When you have a relationship to the largest nest of being home, it is possible to invoke that belonging and navigate anyplace you stand. This is done by remembering the nests of your body, mind, and energetic anatomy and that you have tools of connection in your fibers. You can reach across any distance to the support of the earth and nature if you remember your *basics* and start by finding *ground.*

At Home with People and Sharing Spaces

In reality, you encounter other people in many layers of your nested homes. They might be invited into your energetic space as well as the nest of house and belongings. On the other hand, they might be intrusive! As above, keeping good *basics* in place, especially your edges, makes this dance easier to manage.

The art of relating to people at the energetic level is complex, and I refer you to works by Brennan, *Hands of Light* and *Light Emerging,* for more detail. Even so, there are some practical ways to approach sharing your space. In my work as an organizer helping individual and families in their homes and offices, I've found that being at home with other people is both enriching and challenging.

You can start with three factors that are at the heart of any shared space: communication, territory, and compromise. Each person needs to understand their own relationship to an object or feature of their environment. Until they can communicate about it, it's very hard to solve conflicts. By listening to the emotional and sometimes hidden attitudes of a person, some understanding can be reached. Too often, sharing space becomes purely territorial with no real openness to the reality that there are multiple ways to see and value things.

Example: A Couple in an Apartment with Limited Storage

They disagree about how the front hall closet should be used, one assuming that coats, boots, gloves, and hats *belong there.* The other person has lots of tall equipment for sports, some of which are professional, and to that person *it is obvious* that the closet is the only place for them. Notice the italics. These reveal sets of belief and history that are not being addressed openly but that underlie the conflict. With some conversation and willingness to reach past an impasse, the pair may discover some emotional or energetic content that makes it easier to accommodate the other. Listening carefully may enable one to hear the other's needs and feelings in a new way.

Perhaps the first feels pushed out by the equipment and feels that they don't share that part of the other's life. Knowing that, the second person might be willing to make the front hall into shared space after all and create room elsewhere. On the other hand, perhaps the sporty one manages to explain that he/she never had such valuable stuff before, and it really needs to be kept vertically. While not delighted, the first person agrees, but expects the sporty person to make room for coats in "their" part of another closet.

By communicating about feelings and revealing assumptions, you can approach the test of any relationship—solving conflict without power struggles. Power struggles imply a winner and a loser. Consider this: you could choose to give way in a situation in which you recognize that your cost is less than the other's. This is progress toward a *mutually supportive problem-solving skill. Whoever cares more gets what they want.*

Assuming you're in a generally trusting and positive relationship, by understanding and giving way in the face of a stronger need, you create the likelihood of being understood and accommodated in turn. This example tidily illustrates all three steps in reaching accord. After communication, the practical next step is designing a solution based on territory. This means facing the reality of the closets and how things can be moved or reordered. It also addresses the *ownership* of each space by identifying which is shared and which is considered private.

The third factor is accepting that all of this requires compromise, willingness to negotiate, and maybe counseling. Some fairly creative solutions are possible, and they may not look anything like your first analysis of what success should be.

One more example: Once upon a time, I was daily outraged by a person's need to empty his pockets on the pristine dining room table. Our communication revealed that this was a gesture of homecoming and made him feel ten pounds lighter at the end of the day. I, in turn, reported feeling assaulted and expected to work around his slovenly dumping ground. That was the communication step.

The territory analysis revealed that he was using shared space to offload, and it made me nuts—far *more* nuts, in fact, than he admitted to feeling relieved by this habit. He had personal territory on his dresser, however, and it was not a problem for me to simply scoop up his pocket leavings and put them on his dresser. The compromise: he got to offload but could not expect me to leave it there. Problem solved!

Moving in the World with Authority and Freedom

The idea that you can belong everywhere depends on a deep level of trust. It also requires a realistic acceptance that things outside your body and mind, while in the nested home of nature and wider world, are not necessarily your friends. The trust is not in some benevolent force that only wants the best for you and all of humanity, because I don't think that's how it all works. I am pointing toward a trust in your own being and ability to measure what you encounter in the world. You must be able to gauge the impact it has on you, as well as yours on it.

With the tools of your *basics* and an understanding of how space works (from chapter 4, the Function, Layout, and Energy section), you can be taught by what you encounter. This is true even when things don't go your way.

Navigating an Unfamiliar System

Changing trains in a strange city is one situation that offers practice in environmental awareness skills—it's full of drama, potential chaos, and great satisfaction. Even if this process is familiar to you, you can probably imagine the stress of facing it for the first time. For each core quality of the environment, I have listed some questions that an experienced traveler might recognize, but they are spelled out to illustrate the depth of information available in every space you occupy.

The breakdown between function, layout, and energy is entirely arbitrary and may be different for each person; this is merely a device for beginning to recognize the content all around you. You are *already* using the skill set everywhere, and by making it conscious, you'll gain even more ease and comfort in the places that are not as simple or familiar. So let's imagine it's time to change trains, using the concepts of spatial awareness.

Function: How use is supported
- Can you grab your baggage fast?
- Are doors between train compartments automatic? Do you need one hand or three?
- Where are the reader boards for current platform assignments?

Layout: How spatial locations are related
- Will your rolling bag make it up the stairs, or do you need the escalator?

- Where are bathrooms, food, or bank machines?
- Are your tickets handy, or are they buried in a pocket of a coat in a backpack?

Energy: What the feeling of the place says
- Do you feel rushed, threatened, or overwhelmed?
- Are there cultural cues or particular hints about how to act?
- Are the sights, sounds, and smells interesting or offensive, and do you know why?

Feeling overwhelmed or anxious in unfamiliar settings, getting distracted by all the strange cues, even when I'm excited and happy, can make functioning smoothly a challenge. If I step into the circumstances with curiosity and willingness to learn from all experiences (mistakes and confusion included), it's much easier to figure out the *function, layout,* and *energy* of the place. In fact, for me one of the joys of travel is this slightly bewildered exhilaration.

Once off the plane in Frankfurt, Germany, the first order of business was figuring out the airport connection to the train. I was traveling with my beloved, and we began by planting ourselves outside the human traffic flow in order to get a sense of the available signage and the *function* of the physical space, as well as the movement of people within it. *Layout* emerged as we followed signs and sometimes floundered about looking for the next one. On the way, we noticed the locations of other services and began to create an internal map of the place.

Cultivating this kind of awareness is a powerful skill, even if I think I'll never be there again. It helps me recall bathroom locations, cash machines, and an information desk. Once we made it to the train connection platform and discovered that there was plenty of time to spare, this internal map made it simple to return to a snack bar and then find our platform again.

Being in a space with awareness requires understanding of the function *I expect* it to support. This gets interesting when people have different ideas about that function. My aforementioned beloved firmly believed that there was plenty of time to get our bags down off the overhead racks and muscle them out the door *after* the train stopped. I wanted to take our cue from the people around us, who were all up and hauling bags down from the racks as soon as each station announcement came over the speakers. If we had sat in our seats until the line of people was out the door and then reached for our bags, we might have wound up at the next stop on the line. Here are several levels of expectation, one to negotiate between people, and one in a social context.

Once we had left the train at our stop, my attention tracked the flow of these same people, again looking for *functional* signage that might point to the inner-city connections. Within the swirling movement all around us, I could see *energetic* information about how to behave in concert with people getting on the escalators or putting tickets back into turnstiles. In some places, I know to form an orderly line, but in others, I'll never get a turn unless I shoulder up to the edges of a crowd and take my first opportunity. Frankfurt was a line-up sort of place, but if I didn't pay attention to my turn, I'd get a pointed verbal reminder from someone nearby.

Being at Home

In each of the nested layers, you have this marvelous opportunity to find yourself and your relationship to your surroundings. This is a radical way of moving about in the world, standing in the place of choice and confidence.

After all, a good set of roots can be taken with you anywhere.

Chapter 9

Radical Homecoming
Reflections on Presence and Environment

At times I feel as if I am spread out over the landscape and inside things and am myself living in every tree, the splashing of the waves, in the clouds and animals that come and in the procession of the seasons. There is nothing . . . with which I am not linked.

—*Memories, Dreams, and Reflections,* by C. G. Jung

There are so many ways to practice the art of being home, as many as there are individuals. Your own experience of the nested layers and how they fit together, along with awareness of your energetic anatomy, forges the link that enables a radical homecoming. In this final chapter, I reflect on some further ways that presence and environment interact. *Being home* is that profound moment when you not only learn from your surroundings, but inform them with your intentions. Look around right now. What needs to shift—the light, your teacup? Or perhaps it's the moment to simply acknowledge that you belong exactly where you are.

Being the Interface

Through the apertures of human anatomy, the architecture of the cosmos enters its sentient home.

—Michael Dames

As an interface with the universe, you serve as a potential home to all you encounter. What are you going to invite in? Clearly there are things, people, places, and experiences that you'd rather not invite to dinner!

By taking up residence in your body and life, by learning the skills of energetic awareness, you have a choice about how much you engage with things. Part of managing this is accepting that your interface with the outside is a constant and ongoing process.

For example, you could think about your life in a body as an escalator ride. Health is not a static state that you can achieve and keep; it's more like walking up a downward-moving escalator. Unless you keep moving with firm purpose, stepping up as best you can, the escalator carries you down whether you like it or not.

So too does time carry you forward to your own ending. You can make the experience last longer, and feel more at the helm of the process, if you manage as much as you can. Healing the body and staying healthy thus require awareness and willingness to "step up" into engagement with your physical body and how you experience your surroundings. This is being the interface.

Over the course of a typical day, there are myriad opportunities to track and adjust your experience. Since you are a reflection of your energy anatomy and will, you can actually control and transform your own perception of reality. If you hold the typical Western attitude that you are a fixed and steady personality, you may find this a bit of a leap. I would rather believe that I *have* a personality that is mine to adjust, just as I have some control over my body. Both are vehicles for the *being that I am,* limited perhaps but not the ultimate definition. This brings me back to the ability to stand in my *basics,* specifically my *core.* When I trust my own *core,* I can see that my self-image is flexible. This can be quite liberating.

Another source of inspiration is *The Path: A Practical Approach to Sorcery,* by Esmeralda Arana. This book manages to combine several of my favorite wisdom paths in a refreshing and practical way. Arana writes from her own experience with humor and candor, while tackling wide-ranging information. She brings together key teachings from Carlos Castaneda's books, Alcoholics Anonymous, and shamanism. Arana refers to one teaching of Castaneda in which the pupil is reminded that warriors have no need to defend what they know to be an arbitrary image and save themselves all sorts of grief.

That's something I'd like to remember more often! Who am I when I am *at home?*

As my personality and identity are mine to adjust as I mature, so also my character evolves. For any change to occur, there must be a connection, a bridge between your experience and the environment. The more you know how and why you react as you do, the better chance you have of creating healthy spaces and relationships.

Character Development

Being the interface between a self and the environment is a lifelong endeavor. Along the way and in the process of working on this book, I have come across a number of systems for becoming aware of who I am and how I function in the world. Here are a few more places to explore as you create your own way of *being home.*

Processing Patterns

This approach has been adapted by the work of many people. It began with Wilhelm Reich's analysis of how character and the body are connected. Much of his work was highly controversial and rejected by mainstream therapists, but one kernel that grew into a lasting idea was that people tend to use particular ways of living inside their bodies. These patterns serve to protect the character and can influence a lot of behavior. Rather them seeing them as defenses, you can think of them as your way of handling anything outside yourself, including your interactions with other people. With practice, you can learn to moderate your own reactions and better understand those of others.

Reich's work was adapted by others and eventually offered by Anodea Judith in a more digestible form for modern minds. I learned about them from Lynda Caesara, in whose hands the patterns are presented as a skill set that makes life both more conscious and easier to manage.

In order to simplify these patterns and avoid labels that carry their own freight of meaning, a small group of friends and I decided to rename them. (I have included the original names in parentheses next to each type for cross-referencing purposes.) We wanted some consistent way to reference our own tendencies of falling back on behaviors coming from unconscious dependence on our default patterns. Barbara Ann Brennan, in *Light Emerging*, makes the point that these patterns do not define your character. Instead they open a window to seeing how you habitually distort who you are when under pressure.

The goal is to understand the role of each one, knowing that they all have both an automatic, ingrained defensive aspect, as well as a "light side." This light side is the healthy and appropriate application of your inherent strengths and abilities of character. The ultimate use of these patterns means that you can access *all* of them in your own character, knowing which type of response best serves your circumstances. With this knowledge, it is possible to come *back home* to your own essence, the *being* part of the equation.

Character Patterns by Shape

Name: Cube *(Rigid)*

Protective Skill: Ability to form effective systems of order, organization, rules, and boundaries.

Light Side: Good with patterns, ideas, mental skills, rhythm, and spatial senses. Cubes can be intuitive and methodical at the same time, prioritize well, and stay focused.

Reactive Fears and Illusions: Inability to recognize feelings and resistance to emotional disorder. Can live in the head and avoid issues by imposing rules at the cost of relationships.

The Challenge: Own and integrate feelings and use the sense of order to help create connections, rather than barriers.

Name: Sphere *(Oral)*

Protective Skill: Nurturing and caring as a way to restore well-being.

Light Side: Loving and compassionate, the sphere is caring and generous and attuned to the experiences of others. They are sensual and playful when feeling safe.

Reactive Fears and Illusions: If unsafe, they will lose all sense of separate self and become unable to reference their core, hold boundaries, or take care of themselves.

The Challenge: Learn to hold and honor their own boundaries and live within their bodies while reclaiming the right to comfort themselves.

Name: Pyramid (*Masochist*)

Protective Skill: Ability to hold *ground* and to do so for those around them. They can stand in their *core* and establish clear boundaries.

Light Side: Respect and protect spaces; they do not invade or impose, and expect others to do the same. They are tolerant, have stamina, know themselves, and keep commitments.

Reactive Fears and Illusions: If unbalanced, the pyramid person loses the ability to claim their space and cannot hold their boundaries and edges or speak up for themselves. They can become very angry and hold it in. Then they become repressed and may then explode.

The Challenge: Appropriate expression of anger is a key skill set for pyramids, as well as willingness to speak up for what they want.

Name: Cloud (*Schizoid*)

Protective Skill: Ability to see behind the scenes and make connections.

Light Side: Intuitive and able to connect with psychic abilities and read energy. They are adaptable and creative and have rich imaginations.

Reactive Fears and Illusions: Under stress, the cloud person can become scattered or distracted or seem disconnected to reality.

The Challenge: To stay present in their body, pay attention to what is happening right here. It is important for the cloud person to own that they can stay here and be at home.

Name: Arrow (*Psychopath*)

Protective Skill: Strong will and clear intentions; they are able to meet challenges and take risks.

Light Side: Powerful will and drive and ability to work energy. They are often athletic and thrive on challenge and independence. Can be charismatic and lead well.

Reactive Fears and Illusions: Self-confidence may lead them to overstep their own limitations, and they may also ignore those of others in the process. Empathy may seem lacking.

The Challenge: Acknowledging their limits and becoming able to ask for help. Learning to ask instead of demand, while honoring other people.

I invite you to have a look at these patterns and see if you recognize your own tendencies. You may very well apply several of these patterns to different situations. When you understand your skills and habitual defenses, you can learn to adjust how you react to circumstances. This is yet another pathway to inhabiting your life.

The Enneagram

Just as the character patterns by shape have a light aspect and a distorted side, the nine points of the enneagram are not rigid categories of character. They have also been given different names by different writers, expressing the particular attitude and background of each person. Some present them as psychological traits or personality types, while others focus on more spiritual qualities. A. H. Almaas does the latter while describing how these nine aspects form a whole and how they interrelate. Rather than encouraging the seeker to focus on individual traits, the real challenge is to understand and integrate the lessons and beauty of each enneagram point.

Here are a few of the ways the enneagram points are defined.

Number	A. H. Almaas	Sandra Maitri	Helen Palmer	Don Riso
1	Perfection	Severity	Perfectionist	Reformer
2	Will	Humility	Giver	Helper
3	Law/Harmony	Veracity	Performer	Status Seeker
4	Origin	Equanimity	Romantic	Artist
5	Omniscience	Nonattachment	Observer	Thinker
6	Faith/Strength	Courage	Trooper	Loyalist
7	Wisdom/Plan	Sobriety	Epicure	Generalist
8	Truth	Innocence	Boss	Leader
9	Love	Action	Mediator	Peacemaker

Almaas and Maitri are connected by the work of Claudio Naranjo and are quite complex, worth intense study. Riso and Palmer are more accessible and are places to start. My hope is that these descriptions will be a teaser, one that will lead you to explore some deeper methods of locating and coming home to the sanctuary of self.

Brain Science and Spatial Perception

Apparently there is a location within the brain, the *parahippocampal place area,* which specializes in recognizing *large structures, as opposed to open spaces.* If this brain location were damaged by a stroke, you would get lost more often because you could no longer recognize whole buildings or landmarks in the space you moved through. You'd still be able identify objects and people, but your experience of the environment would be damaged. Instead you'd learn to track your location with smaller objects, moving from bench to bench in a park, for example.

There may even be a specific brain location for recognizing familiar places and another for processing those that are new or unrecognized. From Sternberg in *Healing Spaces: The Science of Place and Well-Being:* "The pathways between the visual cortex and these brain locations may respond strongly to endorphins, which are activated when a place is attractive. So seeing a favorite restaurant might stimulate one part of the brain, while the unexpected toll booth is registered elsewhere."

She also describes how people navigate a place and deal with changing scenery. Some are wired for landmarks (turn left at the Safeway), and others do better with grids (go to the corner of 1st and James). You may even recognize your style by your level of frustration when given directions in the method you don't like. The neurological background for these differences is described in the book. For example, my preference for a bird's-eye view (a map) serves a different neurological function from one that processes an address.

Even if you aren't all that interested in Sternberg's focus on hospital architecture and healing rates, the science is accessible and the anecdotes are very interesting. Whether Sternberg is describing the different effects of a labyrinth versus a maze or how Walt Disney leads you into the pirate cave, she is pointing toward features of day-to-day life in rooms and cities.

When people are ill, the brain's immune molecules are at work, and it has been seen that memory is sometimes affected during this process. At these times, the body is at work from the inside out to restabilize and foster healing, and outer feedback recedes in importance. The environment does affect how healing proceeds; mental and emotional stressors, like too much sudden loud noise or a sense of being abandoned, can affect the release of chemicals in the brain and create a loop of information that can impede recovery.

In *Self Comes to Mind: Constructing the Conscious Brain,* Antonio Damasio explores how your physical human brain is related to your personal, interior identity; the *you* that feels "at home" . . . or not.

As a neuroscientist, Damasio has spent thirty years researching how the brain works. Chapter 2 mentions what he calls the "misleading intuition" that your mental and emotional experiences are fleeting and insubstantial and that your sense of "self" is somehow a nonphysical phenomenon, maybe in the range of quantum physics or some other system—spiritual or energetic—that takes it outside the range of flesh.

From Damasio:

> That is where having an evolutionary perspective comes in handy. Why do we have a brain in the first place? Not to write books, articles, or plays; not to do science or play music. Brains develop because they are an expedient way of managing life in a body. And why do we, by now, have brains that make minds with selves—conscious minds? Because minds and selves increase the management power of brains; *because they permit a better adaptation of a complex organism to complex environments.*

That last bit is important because it points to how self-awareness helps you create *home.* Far from being formed of insubstantial spirit or even energy, Damasio says the "self" originates from the place where brain and body meet, where flesh and bodily feelings present us with integrated information. In other words, the self-as-identity developed organically from the self-as-body.

We evolved the awareness of a separate self *after* living and evolving in bodies that provided us with a direct connection to the outside. This self-as-body has a mind that governs the running of the body. As we know from modern neuroscience, a lot is going on without our conscious control. Damasio calls this level *unconscious.* In this state, the mind is still taking care of the functioning body, but with no measurable "person."

Damasio has some controversial things to say about animals and people in comas and contends that our simian cousins, cats and dogs, and possibly a few other nonhuman species are conscious in that they clearly show signs of having feelings and awareness of themselves as separate beings.

So how do you as a human become "conscious" of yourself and the environment? Damasio thinks that awareness evolved by resting solidly on your ability to track feelings with your body and integrate the messages with your individual mental brain map. He asserts that body knowledge has made possible the subjective personality that you tend to protect as your identity. Taking this one step further, I see this as reinforcing the concept that your body and identity are flexible and mutable.

Another scientist hot on the trail of personal awareness and its impact on how life works is Dan Siegel, author of *Mindsight*. He says that intuition happens when the brain receives information from the body from the neutral networks in the heart and intestines. Somehow we know that we didn't "think" this content, but where does it come from? Traditionally, we have let intuition be a mystery of the human condition, when actually it is grounded in the body itself. The brain is tracking the neural network as a whole and provides our minds with data from systems we typically overlook. This may be the source of the phrase "having a gut feeling." We ignore these messages at our own peril.

What I take from these ideas is that our separate unique beingness in the world is informed by our ability to decode the messages from outside. These messages are the experience of the body in space and are less moderated by intellectual constructs of the personality. We ignore volumes of information that actually connect us to the spaces and places we live in.

This kind of awareness provides clues that can make our lives in the environment much more enjoyable and productive. Being able to make ourselves at home hinges on recognizing when our living spaces have been forced into patterns and shapes (the formal living room) with no regard for how we feel about them or how we really inhabit our private space. At this point in our evolution, we may need to step around or through our mental constructs and maps in order to hear the information all around us!

You are crossing the bridge between inside and outside when your internal maps change your environment. A mental image of a clean desk can begin to change the way you process paper when you create space and discover bills to pay. It works both ways; the images you take in via your senses can also trigger changes to those interior mental maps. You see the tidy stack of action items, and your self-image gradually changes; *you are in control!* Awareness itself is the bridge.

Welcome Back: Being at Home in All Places

My efforts to describe *being home* in a practical way, a way that can be learned and used, have evolved over years of working with the stuff of daily living. Running deeply next to the clutter and organization issues is a stream of personal spiritual endeavor. There is no easy way to thread these together for a large audience, but I hope I have managed to bring them closer.

Psychologists and architects have their own theories and systems about how we understand and react to our environments. Winifred Gallagher's *House Thinking* explores the typical rooms in an American house. She returns repeatedly to the question: Does this room help me to be who I really am?

Culture defines much of your reaction to spaces and the use you make of them. The Hopi tribes of the southwestern United States use a chamber called a kiva for sacred gatherings that many modern city dwellers would see as a hole in the ground. In the same way, a typical upscale bathroom or kitchen in a subdivision home would scream "waste" and "self-absorption" in some developing countries. And yet for many Americans, the master bath is a sacred

right of any adult homeowner. What makes a space sacred is awareness of your being and your relationship to that space. Anyplace
can be a kiva.

In *House Thinking,* Gallagher speaks of the "aedicule" of a home.
This Latin term originally referred to a miniature house or shrine.
It was often imagined as a hearth surrounded by four posts or col-
umns, which was the spiritual center of the home. An aedicule can
be a seating arrangement before the fire, but it can also be a bay
window or the breakfast nook or the objects on a table. By recognizing or making such a focal point in our homes, we can begin to
take ownership of the energy in our environments.

Another way to fine-tune your home is to create focal points
for what you value, honor, or otherwise choose to remember as life
unfolds. Known as an altar in some traditions, it can be a tool for
prayer, a place to commune with ancestors or your own intentions.
Altars can be constructed to direct your attention on your *core* or
on specific goals. How you go about designing one is a personal
process, but know that it can start with any small act of focus, like
lighting a candle or placing a stone on the windowsill. In my home,
practically everything I lay eyes on is an altar of some sort, even if
only to my own pleasure in a memory. In this way, everywhere I
go is kiva.

In *The Unfolding Now,* A. H. Almaas builds a series of concepts
that are a cumulative meditation on awareness. I will briefly sum-
marize. The two parts of human experience are:

1. a central event that arises in your personal experience, and
2. a secondary part composed of your responses and reactions
   to that central event.

How these two components feel and develop is determined by
three processes, or abilities:

1. having a practice of awareness and an ongoing inquiry into being present,

2. cultivating a practice that reveals presence at the heart of all experience, and

3. living with this inquiry, awareness, and experience as it unfolds in all circumstances.

Living with this degree of intimacy with your surroundings allows the false sense of exile to fall away. You are not only here, right now, you are part of it all, separated only by the activity of what you think. If you identify only with your mind and stories that define you, you're cut off from circumstances and where you stand. True presence doesn't separate being and environment. Instead, I invite you to explore a world where you are entirely at home.

Coming full circle, I want to repeat the words from David Foster Wallace's speach.

There are these two young fish swimming along, and they happen to meet an older fish swimming the other way, who nods at them and says, "Morning, boys, how's the water?" And the two young fish swim on for a bit, and then eventually one of them looks over at the other and goes, "What the hell is water?"

His talk concludes with:

Awareness of what is so real and essential, so hidden in plain sight all around us, that we have to keep reminding ourselves over and over: this is water, this is water. It is unimaginably hard to do this, to stay conscious and alive, day in and day out.

Welcome home; please enjoy the water.

Acknowledgments

Many people have made this book possible. My thanks go to Jean Haner, who encouraged my departure from limited ideas of what was possible; Russ Taylor, for repeatedly asking when the book was coming; and Lynda Caesara, for her wisdom and patience. Whom do I leave out? Not my early readers: Anita Boser, Deb Berger, Donna Lough, Kalika Robinson, Mae Waldron, and Rose Harrow. Your confidence in the process was crucial. To Waverly Fitzgerald I owe unending gratitude for her generous advice and teaching about writing and publishing.

Without the unwavering support of my husband, Chris Nielsen, it would have been terribly tedious. I think we'll stay home tonight.

Bibliography

Arana, Esmeralda. *The Path: A Practical Approach to Sorcery.* New York: True Mind, 2004.

Ardalan, Nader, and Laleh Bakhtiar. *The Sense of Unity: The Sufi Tradition in Persian Architecture.* Chicago: University of Chicago, 1973.

Almaas, A. H. *Facets of Unity: The Enneagram of Holy Ideas.* Berkeley, CA: Diamond, 1998.

———. *The Unfolding Now: Realizing Your True Nature through the Practice of Presence.* Boston: Shambhala, 2008.

Berliner, Helen. *Enlightened by Design: Using Contemplative Wisdom to Bring Peace, Wealth, Warmth, and Energy into Your Home.* Boston: Shambhala, 1999.

Brennan, Barbara Ann. *Hands of Light: A Guide to Healing through the Human Energy Field.* Toronto: Bantam, 1987.

———. *Light Emerging: The Journey of Personal Healing.* New York: Bantam, 1993.

Bridges, Carol. *A Soul in Place: Reclaiming Home as Sacred Space.* Nashville, IN: Earth Nation Pub., 1995.

Bryner, Andy, and Dawna Markova. *An Unused Intelligence: Physical Thinking for 21st Century Leadership.* Berkeley, CA: Conari, 1996.

Buber, Martin. *Tales of the Hassidim.* New York: Shocken, 1947.

Busch, Akiko. *Geography of Home: Writings on Where We Live.* New York: Princeton Architectural, 1999.

Colebrook, Joan. *A House of Trees: Memoirs of an Australian Girlhood.* New York: Farrar Straus Giroux, 1987.

Cruden, Loren. *Spirit of Place: A Workbook for Sacred Alignment.* Rochester, VT: Destiny, 1995.

Damasio, Antonio R. *Self Comes to Mind: Constructing the Conscious Brain.* New York: Pantheon, 2010.

Daum, Meghan. *Life Would Be Perfect If I Lived in That House.* New York: Alfred A. Knopf, 2010.

Frost, Randy O., and Gail Steketee. *Stuff: Compulsive Hoarding and the Meaning of Things.* Boston: Houghton Mifflin Harcourt, 2010.

Gallagher, Winifred. *House Thinking: A Room-by-Room Look at How We Live.* New York: HarperCollins, 2006.

Gibson, Katherine. *Unclutter Your Life: Transforming Your Physical, Mental, and Emotional Space.* Hillsboro, OR: Beyond Words Pub., 2004.

Hoffman, Eva. *Lost in Translation: A Life in a New Language.* New York: E.P. Dutton, 1989.

———. *Time.* New York: Picador, 2009.

Judith, Anodea. *Eastern Body, Western Mind: Psychology and the Chakra System as a Path to the Self.* New York: Celestial Arts, 1996.

Lethaby, W. R. *Architecture, Mysticism, and Myth.* New York: G. Braziller, 1975.

Lipton, Bruce H. *The Biology of Belief: Unleashing the Power of Consciousness, Matter, and Miracles.* Santa Rosa, CA: Mountain of Love/Elite, 2005.

Maitri, Sandra. *The Spiritual Dimension of the Enneagram: Nine Faces of the Soul.* New York: Jeremy P. Tarcher/Putnam, 2000.

Marcus, Clare Cooper. *House as a Mirror of Self: Exploring the Deeper Meaning of Home.* Berkeley, CA: Conari, 1995.

McTaggart, Lynne. *The Intention Experiment: Using Your Thoughts to Change Your Life and the World.* New York: Free Press, 2007.

Medina, John. *Brain Rules: 12 Principles for Surviving and Thriving at Work, Home, and School.* Seattle: Pear, 2008.

Moran, Victoria. *Shelter for the Spirit: Create Your Own Haven in a Hectic World.* New York: HarperPerennial, 1998.

Morgenstern, Julie. *When Organizing Isn't Enough: SHED Your Stuff, Change Your Life.* New York: Fireside, 2008.

Naranjo, Claudio. *Character and Neurosis: An Integrative View.* Nevada City, CA: Gateways/IDHHB, 1994.

Norris, Gunilla, and Greta Sibley. *Being Home: A Book of Meditations.* New York: Bell Tower, 1991.

Palmer, Brooks. *Clutter Busting: Letting Go of What's Holding You Back.* Novato, CA: New World Library, 2009.

Palmer, Helen. *The Enneagram in Love and Work: Understanding Your Intimate and Business Relationships.* San Francisco: HarperSanFrancisco, 1995.

Peirce, Penney. *Frequency: The Power of Personal Vibration.* New York: Atria, 2009.

Plotkin, Bill. *Soulcraft: Crossing into the Mysteries of Nature and Psyche.* Novato, CA: New World Library, 2003.

Pogacnik, Marko. *Sacred Geography: Geomancy—Co-creating the Earth Cosmos*. Great Barrington, MA: Lindisfarne, 2007.

Powning, Beth. *Home: Chronicle of a North Country Life*. New York: Stewart, Tabori & Chang, 1996.

Rich, Mark, and Gosha Karpowicz. *Energetic Anatomy: An Illustrated Guide to Understanding and Using the Human Energy System*. Ashland, OR: Wave of the Future, 2004.

Riso, Don Richard. *Personality Types: Using the Enneagram for Self-Discovery*. Boston: Houghton Mifflin, 1987.

Robyn, Kathryn L. *Spiritual Housecleaning: Healing the Space within by Beautifying the Space around You*. Oakland, CA: New Harbinger Publications, 2001.

Rufus, Anneli S. *Stuck: Why We Can't (or Won't) Move On*. New York: Tarcher/Penguin, 2008.

Siegel, Daniel J. *Mindsight: The New Science of Personal Transformation*. New York: Bantam, 2010.

Sternberg, Esther M. *Healing Spaces: The Science of Place and Well-Being*. Cambridge, MA: Belknap of Harvard UP, 2009.

Susanka, Sarah. *The Not So Big Life: Making Room for What Really Matters*. New York: Random House, 2007.

Taylor, Jill Bolte. *My Stroke of Insight: A Brain Scientist's Personal Journey*. New York: Viking, 2008.

Thorp, Gary. *Sweeping Changes: Discovering the Joy of Zen in Everyday Tasks*. New York: Walker & Co., 2000.

Vogt, Stephanie Bennett. *Your Spacious Self: Clear the Clutter and Discover Who You Are*. San Antonio, TX: Hierophant Publishing, 2012.

Waggoner, Robert. *Lucid Dreaming: Gateway to the Inner Self*. Needham, MA: Moment Point, 2009.

Wallace, David Foster. "David Foster Wallace on Life and Work." Commencement Address. Gambier, OH: Kenyon College, 2005.

Walsh, Peter. *Enough Already! Clearing Mental Clutter to Become the Best You*. New York: Free Press, 2009.

Zander, Rosamund Stone, and Benjamin Zander. *The Art of Possibility*. Boston: Harvard Business School, 2000.

Zimbardo, Philip, and John Boyd. *The Time Paradox: The New Psychology of Time and How It Will Change Your Life*. New York: Free Press, 2008.

About the Author

Rebecca Ross grew up wanting to know why some houses felt better than others. Helping people in their real spaces became Rebecca's mission. In 2000, after twenty years as an architect, she founded The Composed Domain, which melds her architecture background, her understanding of spatial energy, and her skill at organizing things and information. As a professional organizer, she works directly with home and business owners in their spaces to reduce clutter, restore balance, and enhance well-being. She teaches classes, speaks at ADD and OCD support groups, and has appeared on local Seattle NPR station KUOW and the KING 5 *New Day Northwest* morning show. She was also featured on three episodes of TLC's hit reality TV show *Hoarding: Buried Alive*. Rebecca has become a specialist in hoarding and chronic acquiring, partnering with Seattle-area therapists to support people dealing with serious issues.

Visit her online at: www.composedomain.com.